EIGHTY-NINTH EDITION

Manual of The Mother Church
The First Church of Christ
Scientist
in Boston, Massachusetts

BY

MARY BAKER EDDY

DISCOVERER AND FOUNDER OF CHRISTIAN SCIENCE, AND AUTHOR
OF THE CHRISTIAN SCIENCE TEXTBOOK, "SCIENCE AND
HEALTH WITH KEY TO THE SCRIPTURES"

Registered
U. S. Patent Office

PUBLISHED BY THE
TRUSTEES UNDER THE WILL OF MARY BAKER G. EDDY
BOSTON, U.S.A.

EXTRACT FROM A LETTER IN "MISCEL-
LANEOUS WRITINGS"   *By Mary Baker Eddy*

THE Rules and By-Laws in the Manual
of The First Church of Christ, Scientist,
Boston, originated not in solemn con-
clave as in ancient Sanhedrim. They
were not arbitrary opinions nor dictatorial demands,
such as one person might impose on another. They
were impelled by a power not one's own, were
written at different dates, and as the occasion required. They sprang from necessity, the logic of
events,—from the immediate demand for them as
a help that must be supplied to maintain the dignity
and defense of our Cause; hence their simple,
scientific basis, and detail so requisite to demonstrate genuine Christian Science, and which will do
for the race what absolute doctrines destined for
future generations might not accomplish.

Table of Contents

TENETS 15

HISTORICAL SKETCH 17

LIST OF CHURCH OFFICERS 21

Church By-Laws

CHURCH OFFICERS

Names, Election, and Duties. Art. I
Names 25
President 25
Clerk and Treasurer 25
Readers 26
Directors 26
Church Business 27
Publishing Buildings 27
Trusteeships and Syndicates 27
Duties of Church Officers 28

Readers of The Mother Church. Art. II
Election 29
Eligibility 30
Removal 30
First Reader's Residence 30

DUTIES OF READERS OF THE MOTHER CHURCH AND
OF ITS BRANCH CHURCHES. ART. III

Moral Obligations 31
First Readers' Duties 31
Suitable Selections 31
Order of Reading 32
Naming Book and Author 32
Readers in Branch Churches 32
Enforcement of By-Laws 32
A Reader not a Leader 33

CHURCH MEMBERSHIP

QUALIFICATIONS FOR MEMBERSHIP. ART. IV

Believe in Christian Science 34
Free from Other Denominations 34
Children when Twelve Years Old 35

APPLICATIONS FOR MEMBERSHIP. ART. V

Students of the College 35
Other Students 35
Students' Pupils 36
Exceptional Cases 36
Addressed to Clerk 36
Endorsing Applications 37
Notice of Rejection 37

RECOMMENDATION AND ELECTION. ART. VI

Pupils of Normal Students 37
Members of The Mother Church 37
Election 38

PROBATIONARY MEMBERSHIP. ART. VII

Members who once Withdrew 38
Members once Dismissed 39
Ineligible for Probation 39

DISCIPLINE

GUIDANCE OF MEMBERS. ART. VIII

A Rule for Motives and Acts 40
To be Read in Church 40
Christ Jesus the Ensample 41
Daily Prayer 41
Prayer in Church 42
Alertness to Duty 42
One Christ 42
No Malpractice 42
Formulas Forbidden 43
No Adulterating Christian Science 43
No Incorrect Literature 43
Obnoxious Books 44
Per Capita Tax 44
Church Periodicals 44
Church Organizations Ample 44
Joining Another Society 45
Forbidden Membership 45
Officious Members 45
Legal Titles 45
Illegal Adoption 46
Use of Initials "C. S." 46
Practitioners and Patients 46
Duty to Patients 47
Testimonials 47
Charity to All 47
Uncharitable Publications 48
The Golden Rule 48
Numbering the People 48
Our Church Edifices 48

No Monopoly 49
Christian Science Nurse 49

MARRIAGE AND DECEASE. ART. IX
A Legal Ceremony 49
Sudden Decease 49

DEBATING IN PUBLIC. ART. X
No Unauthorized Debating 50

COMPLAINTS. ART. XI
Departure from Tenets 50
Violation of By-Laws 50
Violation of Christian Fellowship 51
Preliminary Requirement 51
Authority 51
Members in Mother Church Only 52
Working Against the Cause 52
No Unchristian Conduct 53
Not to Learn Hypnotism 53
Publications Unjust 53
The Mother Church of Christ, Scientist, Tenets . . . 54
Special Offense 54
Members of Branch Churches 54

TEACHERS. ART. XII
Probation 55
Misteaching 55

MEETINGS

REGULAR AND SPECIAL MEETINGS. ART. XIII
Annual Meetings 56
Meetings of Board of Directors 56
Called only by the Clerk 57

CHURCH SERVICES

THE CHRISTIAN SCIENCE PASTOR. ART. XIV
Ordination 58
The Lesson-Sermon 58

READING IN PUBLIC. ART. XV
Announcing Author's Name 58

WELCOMING STRANGERS. ART. XVI
The Leader's Welcome 59
The Local Members' Welcome 59

SERVICES UNINTERRUPTED. ART. XVII
Continued Throughout the Year 60
Easter Observances 60
Laying a Corner Stone 60
Overflow Meetings 61

COMMUNION. ART. XVIII
No More Communion 61
Communion of Branch Churches 61

MUSIC IN THE CHURCH. ART. XIX
Soloist and Organist 61

SUNDAY SCHOOL. ART. XX
The Sunday School 62
Teaching the Children 62
Subject for Lessons 62

READING ROOMS. ART. XXI
Establishment 63
Librarian 63
Literature in Reading Rooms 64

RELATION AND DUTIES OF MEMBERS TO
PASTOR EMERITUS. Art. XXII

The Title of Mother Changed 64
A Member not a Leader 65
Obedience Required 65
Understanding Communications 65
Interpreting Communications 66
Reading and Attesting Letters 66
Unauthorized Reports 66
Private Communications 67
Unauthorized Legal Action 67
Duty to God 67
Opportunity for Serving the Leader 67
Location 68
Agreement Required 68
Incomplete Term of Service 69
Help 69
Students with Mrs. Eddy 69
Mrs. Eddy's Room 69
Pastor Emeritus to be Consulted 70

THE MOTHER CHURCH AND BRANCH
CHURCHES. Art. XXIII

Local Self-government 70
Titles 70
Mother Church Unique 71
Tenets Copyrighted 71
Manual 72
Organizing Churches 72
Requirements for Organizing Branch Churches . . . 72
Privilege of Members 73
No Close Communion 73

No Interference   73
Teachers' and Practitioners' Offices   74
Recognition   74

GUARDIANSHIP OF CHURCH FUNDS. Art.
    XXIV

Church Edifice a Testimonial   75
Financial Situation   75
Report of Directors   76
Finance Committee   76
God's Requirement   77
Provision for the Future   77
Debt and Duty   78
Emergencies   78
Committee on Business   79

THE CHRISTIAN SCIENCE PUBLISHING
    SOCIETY. Art. XXV

Board of Trustees   79
Disposal of Funds   80
Vacancies in Trusteeship   80
Editors and Manager   80
Suitable Employees   81
Periodicals   81
Rule of Conduct   81
Books to be Published   81
Removal of Cards   82

TEACHING CHRISTIAN SCIENCE

Teachers. Art. XXVI
Motive in Teaching   83
Care of Pupils   83
Defense against Malpractice   84

Number of Pupils 84

Pupil's Tuition 84

Associations 84

A Single Field of Labor 84

Caring for Pupils of Strayed Members 85

Teachers must have Certificates 85

PUPILS. ART. XXVII

Authorized to Teach 86

Without Teachers 86

Basis for Teaching 86

Church Membership 87

Class Teaching 87

BOARD OF EDUCATION

ORGANIZATION. ART. XXVIII

Officers 88

Election 88

President not to be Consulted 88

Presidency of College 89

APPLICANTS AND GRADUATES. ART. XXIX

Normal Teachers 89

Qualifications 89

Certificates 90

ACTION OF THE BOARD. ART. XXX

Sessions 90

Special Instruction 90

Signatures 91

Remuneration and Free Scholarship 91

Surplus Funds 91

Primary Students 91

Healing Better than Teaching 92
Not Members of The Mother Church 92

BOARD OF LECTURESHIP

ORGANIZATION AND DUTIES. ART. XXXI

Election 93
Duty of Lecturers 93
No Disruption of Branch Churches 93
Receptions 94
Circuit Lecturer 94

CALLS FOR LECTURES. ART. XXXII

From the Directors 95
From Branch Churches 95
From Societies 95
Annual Lectures 95
No Lectures by Readers 95
No Wednesday Evening Lectures 96
Lecture Fee 96
Expenses 96
Exceptional Cases 96

COMMITTEE ON PUBLICATION. ART. XXXIII

In The Mother Church 97
Duties 97
In Branch Churches 98
Appointment 99
Removal from Office 100
Case of Necessity 100

CHURCH–BUILDING. ART. XXXIV

Building Committee 102
Designation of Deeds 102
The Mother Church Building 103

CHURCH MANUAL. Art. XXXV

    For The Mother Church Only 104

    Seventy-third Edition the Authority 104

    Amendment of By-Laws 105

Appendix

Special Instructions Regarding Applications for
    Church Membership 109

Present Order of Services in The Mother Church
    and Branch Churches 120

Present Order of Communion Services in Branch
    Churches 125

Order of Exercises for the Sunday School of The
    Mother Church and Branch Churches 127

Deed of Trust 128

Deed Conveying Land for Church Purposes 136

Tenets

of The Mother Church
The First Church of Christ, Scientist

To be signed by those uniting with The First   1
Church of Christ, Scientist, in Boston, Mass.

1. As adherents of Truth, we take the inspired   3
Word of the Bible as our sufficient guide to eternal
Life.

2. We acknowledge and adore one supreme and   6
infinite God. We acknowledge His Son, one Christ;
the Holy Ghost or divine Comforter; and man in
God's image and likeness.   9

3. We acknowledge God's forgiveness of sin in
the destruction of sin and the spiritual understanding
that casts out evil as unreal. But the belief in sin is   12
punished so long as the belief lasts.

4. We acknowledge Jesus' atonement as the evidence of divine, efficacious Love, unfolding man's   15
unity with God through Christ Jesus the Way-shower;

1 and we acknowledge that man is saved through Christ,
through Truth, Life, and Love as demonstrated by the
3 Galilean Prophet in healing the sick and overcoming
sin and death.

5. We acknowledge that the crucifixion of Jesus
6 and his resurrection served to uplift faith to understand eternal Life, even the allness of Soul, Spirit, and
the nothingness of matter.

9   6. And we solemnly promise to watch, and pray
for that Mind to be in us which was also in Christ
Jesus; to do unto others as we would have them do
12 unto us; and to be merciful, just, and pure.

MARY BAKER EDDY

Historical Sketch

IN THE spring of 1879, a little band of earnest   1
seekers after Truth went into deliberations over
forming a church without creeds, to be called the   3
" CHURCH OF CHRIST, SCIENTIST." They were members of evangelical churches, and students of Mrs.
Mary Baker Eddy in Christian Science, and were   6
known as " Christian Scientists."

At a meeting of the Christian Scientist Association,
April 12, 1879, on motion of Mrs. Eddy, it was   9
voted, — To organize a church designed to com-
memorate the word and works of our Master, which
should reinstate primitive Christianity and its lost   12
element of healing.

Mrs. Eddy was appointed on the committee to
draft the Tenets of The Mother Church — the chief   15
corner stone whereof is, that Christian Science, as
taught and demonstrated by our Master, casts out
error, heals the sick, and restores the lost Israel: 18

1 for " the stone which the builders rejected, the same
is become the head of the corner."

3   The charter for the Church was obtained June,
1879,* and the same month the members, twenty-six
in number, extended a call to Mary Baker Eddy
6 to become their pastor.   She accepted the call,
and was ordained A. D. 1881.   Although walking
through deep waters, the little Church went steadily
9 on, increasing in numbers, and at every epoch
saying,

    " Hitherto hath the Lord helped us."

12   On the twenty-third day of September, 1892, at
the request of Rev. Mary Baker Eddy, twelve
of her students and Church members met and re-
15 organized, under her jurisdiction, the Christian
Science Church and named it, THE FIRST CHURCH
OF CHRIST, SCIENTIST.

18   At this meeting twenty others of Mrs. Eddy's
students and members of her former Church were
elected members of this Church, — those with others
21 that have since been elected were known as " First
Members."   The Church Tenets, Rules, and By-
Laws, as prepared by Mrs. Eddy, were adopted.   A
24 By-Law adopted March 17, 1903, changed the
title of " First Members " to " Executive Members."
(On July 8, 1908, the By-Laws pertaining to " Ex-
27 ecutive Members " were repealed.)

THE FIRST CHURCH OF CHRIST, SCIENTIST, IN BOS-   1
TON, MASS., is designed to be built on the Rock,
Christ; even the understanding and demonstration   3
of divine Truth, Life, and Love, healing and saving
the world from sin and death; thus to reflect in some
degree the Church Universal and Triumphant.   6

* Steps were taken to promote the Church of Christ, Scientist, in
April, May and June; formal organization was accomplished and the
charter obtained in August, 1879.

CHURCH OFFICERS

Rev. MARY BAKER EDDY
Pastor Emeritus

GEORGE WENDELL ADAMS
CHARLES E. HEITMAN
Mrs. NELVIA E. RITCHIE
W. STUART BOOTH
FRANCIS LYSTER JANDRON

} Christian Science Board
of Directors

Mrs. ELISABETH F. NORWOOD
President

GORDON V. COMER
Temporary First Reader
Conducts services and reads from the Christian Science
textbook,
"SCIENCE AND HEALTH WITH KEY TO THE
SCRIPTURES"
By Mary Baker Eddy

Miss MARGARET CRAWFORD
Second Reader
Reads from the SCRIPTURES

Miss MARY G. EWING
Clerk, 107 Falmouth Street,
Boston, Mass.

ROY GARRETT WATSON
Treasurer, 107 Falmouth Street, Boston, Mass.

1942–1943

Church By-Laws

Church By-Laws

CHURCH OFFICERS

ARTICLE I

NAMES, ELECTION, AND DUTIES

Names. SECTION 1. The Church officers shall consist of the Pastor Emeritus, a Board of Directors, a President, a Clerk, a Treasurer, and two [6] Readers.

President. SECT. 2. The President shall be elected, subject to the approval of the Pastor [9] Emeritus, by the Board of Directors [1] on Monday preceding the annual meeting of the Church. The President shall hold office for one [12] year, and the same person is eligible for election but once in three years.

Clerk and Treasurer. SECT. 3. The term of [15] office for the Clerk and the Treasurer of this

---

1 See under " Deed of Trust " for incorporation of the " Christian Science Board of Directors."

1 Church (also for the editors and the manager
of The Christian Science Publishing Society,
3 and the manager of the general Committee on
Publication in Boston) is one year each, dating
from the time of election to office. Incumbents
6 who have served one year or more, may be re-
elected, or new officers elected, at the annual
meeting held for this purpose, by a unanimous
9 vote of the Christian Science Board of Directors and the consent of the Pastor Emeritus
given in her own handwriting.

12   **Readers.** Sect. 4. Every third year Readers shall be elected in The Mother Church by
the Board of Directors, which shall inform the
15 Pastor Emeritus of the names of its candidates
before they are elected; and if she objects, said
candidates shall not be chosen. The Directors
18 shall fix the salaries of the Readers.

Directors. Sect. 5. The Christian Science
Board of Directors shall consist of five members.
21 They shall fill a vacancy occurring on that Board
after the candidate is approved by the Pastor
Emeritus. A majority vote or the request of
24 Mrs. Eddy shall dismiss a member. Members
shall neither report the discussions of this Board,
nor those with Mrs. Eddy.

Church Business. SECT. 6. The business of The Mother Church shall be transacted by its Christian Science Board of Directors. The manager of the general Committee on Publication in the United States shall order no special action to be taken by said Committee that is not named in the Manual of this Church without consulting with the full Board of Directors of The Mother Church and receiving the written consent of said Board.

Publishing Buildings. SECT. 7. It shall be the duty of the Christian Science Board of Directors to provide a suitable building for the publication of *The Christian Science Journal, Christian Science Sentinel, Der Herold der Christian Science,* and all other Christian Science literature published by The Christian Science Publishing Society. It shall also be the duty of the Christian Science Board of Directors to provide suitable rooms, conveniently and pleasantly located in the same building, for the publication and sale of the books of which Mary Baker Eddy is, or may be, the author, and of other literature connected therewith.

Trusteeships and Syndicates. SECT. 8. Boards of Trustees and Syndicates may be

1 formed by The Mother Church, subject to the
approval of the Pastor Emeritus.

3 **Duties of Church Officers.** SECT. 9. Law
constitutes government, and disobedience to the
laws of The Mother Church must ultimate in
6 annulling its Tenets and By-Laws. Without a
proper system of government and form of action, nations, individuals, and religion are un-
9 protected; hence the necessity of this By-Law
and the warning of Holy Writ: " That servant,
which knew his lord's will, and prepared not
12 himself, neither did according to his will, shall
be beaten with many stripes."

It is the duty of the Christian Science Board of
15 Directors to watch and make sure that the officers of this Church perform the functions of
their several offices promptly and well. If an
18 officer fails to fulfil all the obligations of his
office, the Board of Directors shall immediately
call a meeting and notify this officer either to
21 resign his place or to perform his office faithfully; then failing to do either, said officer shall
be dismissed from this Church, and his dismis-
24 sal shall be written on the Church records.

It is the duty of any member of this Church,
and especially of one who has been or who is

the First Reader of a church, to inform the 1
Board of Directors of the failure of the Committee on Publication or of any other officer in 3
this Church to perform his official duties. A
Director shall not make known the name of the
complainant. 6

If the Christian Science Board of Directors fails
to fulfil the requirements of this By-Law, and a
member of this Church or the Pastor Emeritus 9
shall complain thereof to the Clerk and the complaint be found valid, the Directors shall resign
their office or perform their functions faithfully. 12
Failing to do thus, the Pastor Emeritus shall appoint five suitable members of this Church to fill
the vacancy. The salary of the members of the 15
Board of Directors shall be at present two thousand five hundred dollars each annually.

ARTICLE II 18

READERS OF THE MOTHER CHURCH

Election. SECTION 1. The Readers for The
Mother Church shall be a man and a woman, 21
one to read the BIBLE, and one to read SCIENCE
AND HEALTH WITH KEY TO THE SCRIPTURES.

Eligibility. Sect. 2. The Directors shall select intelligible Readers who are exemplary Christians and good English scholars. They must be members of The Mother Church.

Removal. Sect. 3. If a Reader in The Mother Church be found at any time inadequate or unworthy, he or she shall be removed from office by a majority vote of the Board of Directors and the consent of the Pastor Emeritus, and the vacancy supplied.

First Reader's Residence. Sect. 4. Unless Mrs. Eddy requests otherwise, the First Reader of The Mother Church shall occupy, during his term of Readership, the house of the Pastor Emeritus, No. 385 Commonwealth Avenue, Boston. The Board of Directors shall pay from the Church funds the taxes and rent on this property; the Board shall attend to the insurance before it expires, suitably furnish the house, and keep the property in good repair, so long as Mrs. Eddy does not occupy the house herself and the occupants are satisfactory to her.

ARTICLE III   1

DUTIES OF READERS OF THE MOTHER
CHURCH AND OF ITS BRANCH CHURCHES   3

Moral Obligations. SECTION 1. The Readers
of The Mother Church and of all its branch
churches must devote a suitable portion of their   6
time to preparation for the reading of the Sunday
lesson, — a lesson on which the prosperity of
Christian Science largely depends. They must   9
keep themselves unspotted from the world, —
uncontaminated with evil, — that the mental at-
mosphere they exhale shall promote health and   12
holiness, even that spiritual *animus* so universally
needed.

First Readers' Duties. SECT. 2. It shall be   15
the duty of the First Readers to conduct the
principal part of the Sunday services, and the
Wednesday evening meetings.   18

Suitable Selections. SECT. 3. The First
Readers shall read, as a part of the Wednesday
evening services, selections from the SCRIPTURES, 21
and from SCIENCE AND HEALTH WITH KEY TO
THE SCRIPTURES.

1   **Order of Reading.** Sect. 4. The First Readers in the Christian Science churches shall read
3 the correlative texts in Science and Health
with Key to the Scriptures; and the Second
Readers shall read the Bible texts. The readings
6 from the Scriptures shall precede the readings
from Science and Health. The Readers shall
not read from copies or manuscripts, but from
9 the books.

Naming Book and Author. Sect. 5. The
Readers of Science and Health with Key to
12 the Scriptures, before commencing to read
from this book, shall distinctly announce the full
title of the book and give the author's name.
15 Such announcement shall be made but once
during the lesson.

Readers in Branch Churches. Sect. 6.
18 These Readers shall be members of The Mother
Church. They shall read understandingly and
be well educated. They shall make no remarks
21 explanatory of the Lesson-Sermon at any time,
but they shall read all notices and remarks that
may be printed in the Christian Science Quar-
24 terly. This By-Law applies to Readers in all
the branch churches.

Enforcement of By-Laws. Sect. 7. It shall

be the duty of every member of The Mother 1
Church, who is a First Reader in a Church of
Christ, Scientist, to enforce the discipline and 3
by-laws of the church in which he is Reader.

A Reader not a Leader. SECT. 8. The Church
Reader shall not be a Leader, but he shall main- 6
tain the Tenets, Rules, and discipline of the
Church. A Reader shall not be a President of
a church. 9

CHURCH MEMBERSHIP

ARTICLE IV

QUALIFICATIONS FOR MEMBERSHIP

Believe in Christian Science. SECTION 1. To become a member of The Mother Church, The First Church of Christ, Scientist, in Boston, Mass., the applicant must be a believer in the doctrines of Christian Science, according to the platform and teaching contained in the Christian Science textbook, SCIENCE AND HEALTH WITH KEY TO THE SCRIPTURES, by Rev. Mary Baker Eddy. The BIBLE, together with SCIENCE AND HEALTH and other works by Mrs. Eddy, shall be his only textbooks for self-instruction in Christian Science, and for teaching and practising metaphysical healing.

Free from Other Denominations. SECT. 2. This Church will receive a member of another Church of Christ, Scientist, but not a church member from a different denomination until that membership is dissolved.

Children when Twelve Years Old. SECT. 3.
Children who have arrived at the age of twelve
years, who are approved, and whose applications
are countersigned by one of Mrs. Eddy's loyal students, by a Director, or by a student of the Board
of Education, may be admitted to membership
with The Mother Church.

ARTICLE V

APPLICATIONS FOR MEMBERSHIP

Students of the College. SECTION 1. Applications for membership with The Mother Church
from students of the Massachusetts Metaphysical
College who studied with Rev. Mary Baker Eddy,
shall be signed by the Christian Science Board
of Directors as evidence of the loyalty of the
applicants.

Other Students. SECT. 2. Applicants for
membership who have not studied Christian Science with Rev. Mary Baker Eddy, can unite
with this Church only by approval from students
of Mrs. Eddy, loyal to the teachings of the textbook, SCIENCE AND HEALTH WITH KEY TO THE

1 SCRIPTURES, or from members of The Mother
Church, as provided in Article VI, Sect. 2, of
3 these By-Laws.

Students' Pupils. SECT. 3. Applications for
membership with The Mother Church, coming
6 from pupils of loyal students who have taken
the Primary or Normal Course at the Massachusetts Metaphysical College or in the Board
9 of Education, or from pupils of those who have
passed an examination by the Board of Education, shall have the approval and signature of
12 their teachers, except in such cases as are provided for in Sect. 4 of this Article.

Exceptional Cases. SECT. 4. Loyal Chris-
15 tian Scientists whose teachers are deceased, absent, or disloyal, — or those whose teachers, for
insufficient cause, refuse to endorse their appli-
18 cations for membership with The Mother Church,
— can apply to the Clerk of this Church, and
present to him a recommendation signed by three
21 members thereof in good standing, after which,
the unanimous vote of the Board of Directors
may admit said applicant to membership.

24 **Addressed to Clerk.** SECT. 5. All applications for membership must be addressed to the
Clerk of the Church.

Endorsing Applications. SECT. 6. A member of The Mother Church shall not endorse nor countersign an application for membership therewith until after the blank has been properly filled out by an applicant. A member who violates this By-Law shall be disciplined.

Notice of Rejection. SECT. 7. If an application for membership with The First Church of Christ, Scientist, in Boston, Mass., is rejected, the Clerk of the Church shall send to the applicant a notice of such rejection; but neither the Clerk nor the Church shall be obliged to report the cause for rejection.

ARTICLE VI

RECOMMENDATION AND ELECTION

Pupils of Normal Students. SECTION 1. One Normal student cannot recommend the pupil of another Normal student, so long as both are loyal to their Leader and to the Christian Science textbook, except as provided for in Article V, Sect. 4.

Members of The Mother Church. SECT. 2. Only members of The Mother Church are quali-

1 fied to approve for membership individuals who
are known to them to be Christians, and faith-
3 ful, loyal students of the textbook, SCIENCE AND
HEALTH WITH KEY TO THE SCRIPTURES. If the
approver is not a loyal student of Mrs. Eddy, a
6 Director of this Church, or a student of the Board
of Education who holds a degree, the application
must be countersigned by one of these.

9 **Election.** SECT. 3. Applicants for membership in this Church, whose applications are
correctly prepared, may be elected by majority
12 vote of the Christian Science Board of Directors at the semi-annual meetings held for this
purpose.

15   ARTICLE VII

PROBATIONARY MEMBERSHIP

Members who once Withdrew. SECTION 1.
18 Individuals who have heretofore been members
of this Church, or were members of the Church
of Christ, Scientist, organized in 1879 by Mary
21 Baker Eddy, but who have voluntarily with-
drawn, may be received into this Church on one
year's probation, provided they are willing and

anxious to live according to its requirements and make application for membership according to its By-Laws. If, at the expiration of said one year, they are found worthy, they shall be received into full membership, but if not found worthy their applications shall be void.

Members once Dismissed. SECT. 2. A full member or a probationary member, who has been excommunicated once, and who afterward, when sufficient time has elapsed thoroughly to test his sincerity, gives due evidence of having genuinely repented and of being radically reformed, shall be eligible to probationary membership upon a unanimous vote of the Christian Science Board of Directors.

Ineligible for Probation. SECT. 3. If a member has been twice notified of his excommunication, he shall not again be received into this Church.

DISCIPLINE

ARTICLE VIII

GUIDANCE OF MEMBERS

A Rule for Motives and Acts. SECTION 1.
Neither animosity nor mere personal attachment
should impel the motives or acts of the members
of The Mother Church. In Science, divine Love
alone governs man; and a Christian Scientist
reflects the sweet amenities of Love, in rebuk-
ing sin, in true brotherliness, charitableness, and
forgiveness. The members of this Church should
daily watch and pray to be delivered from
all evil, from prophesying, judging, condemning, counseling, influencing or being influenced
erroneously.

To be Read in Church. SECT. 2. The
above Church Rule shall be read in The Mother
Church and in the branch churches by the First
Reader on the first Sunday of each month.
On Communion day the Church Tenets are to
be read.

Christ Jesus the Ensample. SECT. 3. He 1
who dated the Christian era is the Ensample in
Christian Science. Careless comparison or irrev- 3
erent reference to Christ Jesus is abnormal in a
Christian Scientist, and is prohibited. When it is
necessary to show the great gulf between Chris- 6
tian Science and theosophy, hypnotism, or spiritualism, do it, but without hard words. The wise
man saith, "A soft answer turneth away wrath." 9
However despitefully used and misrepresented
by the churches or the press, in return employ
no violent invective, and do good unto your 12
enemies when the opportunity occurs. A departure from this rule disqualifies a member for
office in the Church or on the Board of Lec- 15
tureship, and renders this member liable to discipline and, possibly, dismissal from The Mother
Church. 18

Daily Prayer. SECT. 4. It shall be the duty
of every member of this Church to pray each
day: "Thy kingdom come;" let the reign of 21
divine Truth, Life, and Love be established in
me, and rule out of me all sin; and may Thy
Word enrich the affections of all mankind, and 24
govern them!

1   **Prayer in Church.** SECT. 5. The prayers in
Christian Science churches shall be offered for
3 the congregations collectively and exclusively.

Alertness to Duty. SECT. 6. It shall be the
duty of every member of this Church to defend
6 himself daily against aggressive mental sugges-
tion, and not be made to forget nor to neglect
his duty to God, to his Leader, and to mankind.
9 By his works he shall be judged,— and justified
or condemned.

One Christ. SECT. 7. In accordance with
12 the Christian Science textbooks,— the BIBLE,
and SCIENCE AND HEALTH WITH KEY TO THE
SCRIPTURES,— and in accord with all of Mrs.
15 Eddy's teachings, members of this Church shall
neither entertain a belief nor signify a belief in
more than one Christ, even that Christ whereof
18 the Scripture beareth testimony.

No Malpractice. SECT. 8. Members will not
intentionally or knowingly mentally malpractise,
21 inasmuch as Christian Science can only be practised according to the Golden Rule: "All things
whatsoever ye would that men should do to you,
24 do ye even so to them."   (Matt. 7:12.)

A member of The Mother Church who mentally malpractises upon or treats our Leader or

her staff without her or their consent shall be disciplined, and a second offense as aforesaid shall
cause the name of said member to be dropped
forever from The Mother Church.

Formulas Forbidden. Sect. 9. No member
shall use written formulas, nor permit his patients
or pupils to use them, as auxiliaries to teaching Christian Science or for healing the sick.
Whatever is requisite for either is contained in
the books of the Discoverer and Founder of
Christian Science. Sometimes she may strengthen
the faith by a written text as no one else can.

No Adulterating Christian Science. Sect. 10.
A member of this Church shall not publish
profuse quotations from Mary Baker Eddy's
copyrighted works without her permission, and
shall not plagiarize her writings. This By-Law
not only calls more serious attention to the com-
mandment of the Decalogue, but tends to prevent Christian Science from being *adulterated*.

No Incorrect Literature. Sect. 11. A member of this Church shall neither buy, sell, nor circulate Christian Science literature which is not
correct in its statement of the divine Principle
and rules and the demonstration of Christian
Science. Also the spirit in which the writer

1 has written his literature shall be definitely considered.   His writings must show strict adher-
3 ence to the Golden Rule, or his literature shall
not be adjudged Christian Science. A departure
from the spirit or letter of this By-Law involves
6 schisms in our Church and the possible loss, for
a time, of Christian Science.

Obnoxious Books. SECT. 12. A member of
9 this Church shall not patronize a publishing
house or bookstore that has for sale obnoxious
books.

12   **Per Capita Tax.** SECT. 13. Every member
of The Mother Church shall pay annually a per
capita tax of not less than one dollar, which shall
15 be forwarded each year to the Church Treasurer.

Church Periodicals. SECT. 14. It shall be the
privilege and duty of every member, who can
18 afford it, to subscribe for the periodicals which
are the organs of this Church; and it shall be
the duty of the Directors to see that these period-
21 icals are ably edited and kept abreast of the
times.

Church Organizations Ample. SECT. 15.
24 Members of this Church shall not unite with
organizations which impede their progress in
Christian Science. God requires our whole heart,

and He supplies within the wide channels of The
Mother Church dutiful and sufficient occupation
for all its members.

Joining Another Society. SECT. 16. It shall
be the duty of the members of The Mother
Church and of its branches to promote peace on
earth and good will toward men; but members
of The Mother Church shall not hereafter become members of other societies except those
specified in The Mother Church Manual, and
they shall strive to promote the welfare of all
mankind by demonstrating the rules of divine
Love.

Forbidden Membership. SECT. 17. A member of The First Church of Christ, Scientist, in
Boston, Mass., shall not be a member of any
church whose Readers are not Christian Scientists
and members of The Mother Church.

Officious Members. SECT. 18. A member of
The Mother Church is not entitled to hold office
or read in branch churches of this denomination
except by invitation.

Legal Titles. SECT. 19. Students of Christian Science must drop the titles of Reverend and
Doctor, except those who have received these
titles under the *laws* of the *State*.

1   **Illegal Adoption.** SECT. 20. No person shall
be a member of this Church who claims a spirit-
3 ually adopted child or a spiritually adopted husband or wife. There must be legal adoption and
legal marriage, which can be verified according
6 to the laws of our land.

Use of Initials " C. S." SECT. 21. A member
of The Mother Church shall not place the initials
9 " C. S." after his name on circulars, cards, or
leaflets, which advertise his business or profes-
sion, except as a Christian Science practitioner.

12 **Practitioners and Patients.** SECT. 22. Members of this Church shall hold in sacred confi-
dence all private communications made to them
15 by their patients; also such information as may
come to them by reason of their relation of practitioner to patient. A failure to do this shall sub-
18 ject the offender to Church discipline.

A member of The Mother Church shall not,
under pardonable circumstances, sue his patient
21 for recovery of payment for said member's
practice, on penalty of discipline and liability
to have his name removed from membership.
24 Also he shall reasonably reduce his price in
chronic cases of recovery, and in cases where
he has not effected a cure. A Christian Scientist

is a humanitarian; he is benevolent, forgiving, long-suffering, and seeks to overcome evil with good.

Duty to Patients. SECT. 23. If a member of this Church has a patient whom he does not heal, and whose case he cannot fully diagnose, he may consult with an M. D. on the anatomy involved. And it shall be the privilege of a Christian Scientist to confer with an M. D. on Ontology, or the Science of being.

Testimonials. SECT. 24. "Glorify God in your body, and in your spirit, which are God's" (St. Paul). Testimony in regard to the healing of the sick is highly important. More than a mere rehearsal of blessings, it scales the pinnacle of praise and illustrates the demonstration of Christ, "who healeth all thy diseases" (Psalm 103:3). This testimony, however, shall not include a description of symptoms or of suffering, though the generic name of the disease may be indicated. This By-Law applies to testimonials which appear in the periodicals and to those which are given at the Wednesday evening meeting.

Charity to All. SECT. 25. While members of this Church do not believe in the doctrines of theosophy, hypnotism, or spiritualism, they

1 cherish no enmity toward those who do believe
in such doctrines, and will not harm them.   But
3 whenever God calls a member to bear testimony
to Truth and to defend the Cause of Christ, he
shall do it with love and without fear.

6 **Uncharitable Publications.**   Sect. 26.   A
member of this Church shall not publish, nor
cause to be published, an article that is unchari-
9 table or impertinent towards religion, medicine,
the courts, or the laws of our land.

The Golden Rule.   Sect. 27.   A member of
12 The Mother Church shall not haunt Mrs. Eddy's
drive when she goes out, continually stroll by
her house, or make a summer resort near her
15 for such a purpose.

Numbering the People.   Sect. 28.   Christian
Scientists shall not report for publication the
18 number of the members of The Mother Church,
nor that of the branch churches.   According to
the Scripture they shall turn away from person-
21 ality and numbering the people.

Our Church Edifices.   Sect. 29.   The periodicals of our denomination do not publish de-
24 scriptions of our church edifices, but they may
quote from other periodicals or give incidental
narratives.

No Monopoly. SECT. 30. A Scientist shall not endeavor to monopolize the healing work in any church or locality, to the exclusion of others, but all who understand the teachings of Christian Science are privileged to enter into this holy work, and " by their fruits ye shall know them."

Christian Science Nurse. SECT. 31. A member of The Mother Church who represents himself or herself as a Christian Science nurse shall be one who has a demonstrable knowledge of Christian Science practice, who thoroughly understands the practical wisdom necessary in a sick room, and who can take proper care of the sick.

The cards of such persons may be inserted in *The Christian Science Journal* under rules established by the publishers.

ARTICLE IX

MARRIAGE AND DECEASE

A Legal Ceremony. SECTION 1. If a Christian Scientist is to be married, the ceremony shall be performed by a clergyman who is legally authorized.

Sudden Decease. SECT. 2. If a member of The Mother Church shall decease suddenly, without previous injury or illness, and the cause

4

thereof be unknown, an autopsy shall be made by qualified experts. When it is possible the body of a female shall be prepared for burial by *one of her own sex.*

ARTICLE X

DEBATING IN PUBLIC

No Unauthorized Debating. SECTION 1. A member of this Church shall not debate on Christian Science in public debating assemblies, without the consent of the Board of Directors.

ARTICLE XI

COMPLAINTS

Departure from Tenets. SECTION 1. If a member of this Church shall depart from the Tenets and be found having the name without the life of a Christian Scientist, and another member in good standing shall from Christian motives make this evident, a meeting of the Board of Directors shall be called, and the offender's case shall be tried and said member exonerated, put on probation, or excommunicated.

Violation of By-Laws. SECT. 2. A member who is found violating any of the By-Laws

or Rules herein set forth, shall be admonished
in consonance with the Scriptural demand in
Matthew 18:15–17; and if he neglect to accept
such admonition, he shall be placed on probation,
or if he repeat the offense, his name shall be
dropped from the roll of Church membership.

Violation of Christian Fellowship. SECT. 3.
Any member who shall unjustly aggrieve or
vilify the Pastor Emeritus or another member,
or who does not live in Christian fellowship with
members who are in good and regular standing
with this Church, shall either withdraw from the
Church or be excommunicated.

Preliminary Requirement. SECT. 4. No
Church discipline shall ensue until the requirements according to the Scriptures, in Matthew
18:15–17, have been strictly obeyed, unless a
By-Law governing the case provides for immediate action.

Authority. SECT. 5. The Christian Science
Board of Directors has power to discipline, place
on probation, remove from membership, or to
excommunicate members of The Mother Church.
Only the members of this Board shall be present at meetings for the examination of complaints against Church members; and they alone

1 shall vote on cases involving The Mother Church
discipline.

3 **Members in Mother Church Only.** SECT. 6.
A complaint against a member of The Mother
Church, *if said member belongs to no branch*
6 *church* and if this complaint is not for *mental*
malpractice, shall be laid before this Board, and
within ten days thereafter, the Clerk of the
9 Church shall address a letter of inquiry to the
member complained of as to the validity of
the charge. If a member is found guilty of that
12 whereof he is accused and his previous character
has been good, his confession of his error and
evidence of his compliance with our Church
15 Rules shall be deemed sufficient by the Board
for forgiveness for once, and the Clerk of the
Church shall immediately so inform him. But
18 a second offense shall dismiss a member from
the Church.

Working Against the Cause. SECT. 7. If a
21 member of this Church shall, mentally or otherwise, persist in working against the interests of
another member, or the interests of our Pastor
24 Emeritus and the accomplishment of what she
understands is advantageous to this Church and
to the Cause of Christian Science, or shall influ-

ence others thus to act, upon her complaint or
the complaint of a member for her or for himself,
it shall be the duty of the Board of Directors
immediately to call a meeting, and drop forever
the name of the member guilty of this offense
from the roll of Church membership.

No Unchristian Conduct. Sect. 8. If a
member of this Church were to treat the author
of our textbook disrespectfully and cruelly, upon
her complaint that member should be excommunicated. If a member, without her having re-
quested the information, shall trouble her on
subjects unnecessarily and without her consent,
it shall be considered an offense.

Not to Learn Hypnotism. Sect. 9. Members of this Church shall not learn hypnotism
on penalty of being excommunicated from this
Church. No member shall enter a complaint of
mental malpractice for a sinister purpose. If
the author of Science and Health shall bear
witness to the offense of mental malpractice, it
shall be considered a sufficient evidence thereof.

Publications Unjust. Sect. 10. If a member of The Mother Church publishes, or causes
to be published, an article that is false or unjust,
hence injurious, to Christian Science or to its

Leader, and if, upon complaint by another member, the Board of Directors finds that the offense has been committed, the offender shall be suspended for not less than three years from his or her office in this Church and from Church membership.

The Mother Church of Christ, Scientist, Tenets. SECT. 11. If a member of The Mother Church of Christ, Scientist, or a member of a branch of this Church break the rules of its Tenets as to unjust and unmerciful conduct — on complaint of Mrs. Eddy our Pastor Emeritus — and this complaint being found valid, his or her name shall be erased from The Mother Church and the branch church's list of membership and the offender shall not be received into The Mother Church or a branch church for twelve years.

Special Offense. SECT. 12. If a member of this Church, either by word or work, represents falsely to or of the Leader and Pastor Emeritus, said member shall immediately be disciplined, and a second similar offense shall remove his or her name from membership in The Mother Church.

Members of Branch Churches. SECT. 13. A member of both The Mother Church and a branch

Church of Christ, Scientist, or a Reader, shall not report nor send notices to The Mother Church, or to the Pastor Emeritus, of errors of the members of their local church; but they shall strive to overcome these errors. Each church shall separately and independently discipline its own members, — if this sad necessity occurs.

ARTICLE XII

TEACHERS

Probation. SECTION 1. For sufficient reasons it may be decided that a teacher has so strayed as not to be fit for the work of a Reader in church or a teacher of Christian Science. Although repentant and forgiven by the Church and retaining his membership, this weak member shall not be counted loyal till after three years of exemplary character. Then the Board of Directors may decide if his loyalty has been proved by uniform maintenance of the life of a consistent, consecrated Christian Scientist.

Misteaching. SECT. 2. If a member of this Church is found trying to practise or to teach Christian Science contrary to the statement thereof in its textbook, SCIENCE AND HEALTH

1 WITH KEY TO THE SCRIPTURES, it shall be the
duty of the Board of Directors to admonish
3 that member according to Article XI, Sect. 4.
Then, if said member persists in this offense,
his or her name shall be dropped from the roll
6 of this Church.

MEETINGS

ARTICLE XIII

9   REGULAR AND SPECIAL MEETINGS

Annual Meetings. SECTION 1. The regular
meetings of The Mother Church shall be held
12 annually, on Monday following the first Sunday
in June. No other than its officers are required
to be present. These assemblies shall be for
15 listening to the reports of Treasurer, Clerk, and
Committees, and general reports from the Field.

Meetings of Board of Directors. SECT. 2.
18 The annual meeting of the Christian Science
Board of Directors, for electing officers and
other business, shall be held on Monday preced-
21 ing the annual meeting of the Church. Regular
meetings for electing candidates to membership

with The Mother Church, and for the transac- 1
tion of such other business as may properly come
before these meetings, shall be held on the Fri- 3
day preceding the first Sunday in June, and on
the first Friday in November of each year. Special meetings may be held at any time upon the 6
call of the Clerk.

Called only by the Clerk. SECT. 3. Before
calling a meeting of the members of this Church 9
(excepting its regular sessions) it shall be the
duty of the Clerk to inform the Board of Directors and the Pastor Emeritus of his intention, 12
and to state definitely the purpose for which the
members are to convene. The Clerk must have
the consent of this Board and the Pastor Emer- 15
itus, before he can call said meeting.

CHURCH SERVICES

ARTICLE XIV

THE CHRISTIAN SCIENCE PASTOR

Ordination. SECTION 1. I, Mary Baker Eddy, ordain the BIBLE, and SCIENCE AND HEALTH WITH KEY TO THE SCRIPTURES, Pastor over The Mother Church, — The First Church of Christ, Scientist, in Boston, Mass., — and they will continue to preach for this Church and the world.

The Lesson-Sermon. SECT. 2. The subject of the Lesson-Sermon in the morning service of The Mother Church, and of the branch Churches of Christ, Scientist, shall be repeated at the other services on Sunday. The correlative Biblical texts in the Lesson-Sermon shall extend from Genesis to Revelation.

ARTICLE XV

READING IN PUBLIC

Announcing Author's Name. SECTION 1. To pour into the ears of listeners the sacred

revelations of Christian Science indiscriminately, 1
or without characterizing their origin and thus
distinguishing them from the writings of authors 3
who think at random on this subject, is to
lose some weight in the scale of right think-
ing. Therefore it is the duty of every member 6
of this Church, when publicly reading or quot-
ing from the books or poems of our Pastor
Emeritus, first to announce the name of the 9
author. Members shall also instruct their pupils
to adopt the aforenamed method for the benefit
of our Cause. 12

Article XVI

WELCOMING STRANGERS

The Leader's Welcome. Section 1. Mrs. 15
Eddy welcomes to her seats in the church,
persons of all sects and denominations who
come to listen to the Sunday sermon and are 18
not otherwise provided with seats.

The Local Members' Welcome. Sect. 2. It
shall be the duty and privilege of the local mem- 21
bers of The Mother Church to give their seats, if
necessary, to strangers who may come to attend
the morning services. 24

ARTICLE XVII

SERVICES UNINTERRUPTED

Continued Throughout the Year. SECTION 1. The services of The Mother Church shall be continued twelve months each year. One meeting on Sunday during the months of July and August is sufficient. A Christian Scientist is not fatigued by prayer, by reading the Scriptures or the Christian Science textbook. Amusement or idleness is weariness. Truth and Love rest the weary and heavy laden.

Easter Observances. SECT. 2. In the United States there shall be no special observances, festivities, nor gifts at the Easter season by members of The Mother Church. Gratitude and love should abide in every heart each day of all the years. Those sacred words of our beloved Master, " Let the dead bury their dead," and " Follow thou me," appeal to daily Christian endeavors for the living whereby to exemplify our risen Lord.

Laying a Corner Stone. SECT. 3. No large gathering of people nor display shall be allowed when laying the Corner Stone of a Church of Christ, Scientist. Let the ceremony be devout.

No special trowel should be used.   (See Science
and Health, page 140.)

Overflow Meetings.   Sect. 4.   A Church of
Christ, Scientist, shall not hold two or more
Sunday services at the same hour.

Article XVIII

COMMUNION

No more Communion.   Section 1.   The
Mother Church of Christ, Scientist, shall observe
no more Communion seasons.

Communion of Branch Churches.   Sect. 2.
The Communion shall be observed in the branch
churches on the second Sunday in January and
July of each year, and at this service the Tenets
of The Mother Church are to be read.

Article XIX

MUSIC IN THE CHURCH

Soloist and Organist.   Section 1.   The music
in The Mother Church shall not be operatic, but
of an appropriate religious character and of a
recognized standard of musical excellence; it
shall be played in a dignified and suitable manner.   Music from the organ alone should continue about eight or nine minutes for the

1 voluntary and six or seven minutes for the post-
lude, the offertory conforming to the time re-
3 quired to take the collection.   The solo singer
shall not neglect to sing any special hymn selected
by the Board of Directors.

6   ARTICLE XX

                    SUNDAY SCHOOL

The Sunday School. SECTION 1. Pupils may
9 be received in the Sunday School classes of any
Church of Christ, Scientist, up to the age of
twelve years, and by transfer from another
12 Church of Christ, Scientist, up to that age, but
no pupil shall remain in the Sunday School of
any Church of Christ, Scientist, after reaching
15 the age of twenty.   None except the officers,
teachers, and pupils should attend the Sunday
School exercises.

18   **Teaching the Children.** SECT. 2. The
Sabbath School children shall be taught the
Scriptures, and they shall be instructed ac-
21 cording to their understanding or ability to grasp
the simpler meanings of the divine Principle that
they are taught.

24   **Subject for Lessons.** SECT. 3. The first
lessons of the children should be the Ten Com-

mandments (Exodus 20: 3–17), the Lord's Prayer (Matt. 6: 9–13), and its Spiritual Interpretation by Mary Baker Eddy, Sermon on the Mount (Matt. 5: 3–12). The next lessons consist of such questions and answers as are adapted to a juvenile class, and may be found in the Christian Science Quarterly Lessons, read in Church services. The instruction given by the children's teachers must not deviate from the absolute Christian Science contained in their textbook.

READING ROOMS

Article XXI

Establishment. Section 1. Each church of the Christian Science denomination shall have a Reading Room, though two or more churches may unite in having Reading Rooms, provided these rooms are well located.

Librarian. Sect. 2. The individuals who take charge of the Reading Rooms of The Mother Church shall be elected by the Christian Science Board of Directors, subject to the approval of Mary Baker Eddy. He or she shall have no bad habits, shall have had experience in

1 the Field, shall be well educated, and a devout
Christian Scientist.[1]

3 **Literature in Reading Rooms.** SECT. 3. The
literature sold or exhibited in the Reading Rooms
of Christian Science Churches shall consist only
6 of *Science and Health with Key to the Scrip-*
tures, by Mary Baker Eddy, and other writings
by this author; also the literature published or
9 sold by The Christian Science Publishing Society.

RELATION AND DUTIES OF MEM—
BERS TO PASTOR EMERITUS

12   ARTICLE XXII

The Title of Mother Changed. SECTION 1.
In the year eighteen hundred and ninety-five,
15 loyal Christian Scientists had given to the author
of their textbook, the Founder of Christian Science, the individual, endearing term of Mother.
18 At first Mrs. Eddy objected to being called thus,
but afterward consented on the ground that this
appellative in the Church meant nothing more
21 than a tender term such as sister or brother. In
the year nineteen hundred and three and after,
owing to the public misunderstanding of this
24 name, it is the duty of Christian Scientists to

1 See also Article XXV, Sect. 7.

drop the word *mother* and to substitute Leader,   1
already used in our periodicals.

A Member not a Leader.   SECT. 2.   A   3
member of The First Church of Christ, Scientist, in Boston, Mass., shall not be called
Leader by members of this Church, when this   6
term is used in connection with Christian
Science.

Obedience Required.   SECT. 3.   It shall be   9
the duty of the officers of this Church, of the
editors of the *Christian Science Journal, Sen-*
tinel, and *Der Herold,* of the members of the   12
Committees on Publication, of the Trustees of
The Christian Science Publishing Society, and
of the Board of Education promptly to comply   15
with any written order, signed by Mary Baker
Eddy, which applies to their official functions.
Disobedience to this By-Law shall be sufficient   18
cause for the removal of the offending member
from office.

The vacancy shall be supplied by a majority   21
vote of the Christian Science Board of Directors, and the candidate shall be subject to the
approval of Mary Baker Eddy.   24

Understanding Communications.   SECT. 4.
If the Clerk of this Church shall receive a com-

1 munication from the Pastor Emeritus which he
does not fully understand, he shall inform her
3 of this fact before presenting it to the Church
and obtain a clear understanding of the matter,
— then act in accordance therewith.

6 **Interpreting Communications.** SECT. 5. If
at a meeting of this Church a doubt or dis-
agreement shall arise among the members as to
9 the signification of the communications of the
Pastor Emeritus to them, before action is taken
it shall be the duty of the Clerk to report to her
12 the vexed question and to await her explanation
thereof.

Reading and Attesting Letters. SECT. 6.
15 When a letter or a message from the Pastor
Emeritus is brought before a meeting of this
Church, or she is referred to as authority for
18 business, it shall be the duty of the Church to
inquire if all of the letter has been read, and to
require all of it to be read; also to have any
21 authority supposed to come from her satisfactorily attested.

Unauthorized Reports. SECT. 7. Members
24 of this Church shall not report on authority an
order from Mrs. Eddy that she has not sent,
either to the Boards or to the executive bodies

of this Church. The Pastor Emeritus is not to 1
be consulted on cases of discipline, on the cases
of candidates for admission to this Church, or 3
on the cases of those on trial for dismissal from
the Church.

Private Communications. Sect. 8. A strictly 6
private communication from the Pastor Emeritus
to a member of her Church shall not be made
public without her written consent. 9

Unauthorized Legal Action. Sect. 9. A
member of this Church shall not employ an at-
torney, nor take legal action on a case not pro- 12
vided for in its By-Laws — if said case relates
to the person or to the property of Mary Baker
Eddy — without having personally conferred 15
with her on said subject.

Duty to God. Sect. 10. Members of this
Church who turn their attention from the divine 18
Principle of being to personality, sending gifts,
congratulatory despatches or letters to the Pastor
Emeritus on Thanksgiving, Christmas, New Year, 21
or Easter, break a rule of this Church and are
amenable therefor.

Opportunity for Serving the Leader. Sect. 24
11. At the written request of the Pastor Emeritus, Mrs. Eddy, the Board of Directors shall

1 immediately notify a person who has been a
member of this Church at least three years to
3 go in ten days to her, and it shall be the duty
of the member thus notified to remain with Mrs.
Eddy three years consecutively. A member who
6 leaves her in less time without the Directors'
consent or who declines to obey this call to
duty, upon Mrs. Eddy's complaint thereof shall
9 be excommunicated from The Mother Church.
Members thus serving the Leader shall be paid
semi-annually at the rate of one thousand dol-
12 lars yearly in addition to rent and board. Those
members whom she teaches the course in Divin-
ity, and who remain with her three consecutive
15 years, receive the degree of the Massachusetts
Metaphysical College.

Location. SECT. 12. Rev. Mary Baker Eddy
18 calls to her home or allows to visit or to locate
therein only those individuals whom she engages
through the Christian Science Board of Direc-
21 tors of The Mother Church. This By-Law takes
effect on Dec. 15, 1908.

Agreement Required. SECT. 13. When the
24 Christian Science Board of Directors calls a student in accordance with Article XXII, Sect. 11,
of our Church Manual to the home of their

Leader, Mrs. Eddy, said student shall come under
a signed agreement to remain with Mrs. Eddy
if she so desires, during the time specified in the
Church Manual.

Incomplete Term of Service.   Sect. 14.   If a
student who has been called to serve our Leader
in accordance with Article XXII, Sect. 11, of
the Church Manual leaves her before the expiration of the time therein mentioned such student
shall pay to Mrs. Eddy whatsoever she may
charge for what she has taught him or her during the time of such service.

Help.   Sect. 15.   If the author of the Christian Science textbook call on this Board for
household help or a handmaid, the Board shall
immediately appoint a proper member of this
Church therefor, and the appointee shall go immediately in obedience to the call. " He that lov-
eth father or mother more than me is not worthy
of me." (Matt. 10:37.)

Students with Mrs. Eddy.   Sect. 16.   Students employed by Mrs. Eddy at her home shall
not take care of their churches or attend to other
affairs outside of her house.

Mrs. Eddy's Room.   Sect. 17.   The room in
The Mother Church formerly known as " Mother's
Room " shall hereafter be closed to visitors.

1   **Pastor Emeritus to be Consulted.** SECT. 18.
The Mother Church shall not make a church By-
3 Law, nor enter into a business transaction with a
Christian Scientist in the employ of Rev. Mary
Baker Eddy, without first consulting her on said
6 subject and adhering strictly to her advice thereon.

THE MOTHER CHURCH AND
BRANCH CHURCHES

9   ARTICLE XXIII

Local Self-government. SECTION 1.   The
Mother Church of Christ, Scientist, shall assume
12 no general official control of other churches, and
it shall be controlled by none other.

Each Church of Christ, Scientist, shall have its
15 own form of government.   No conference of
churches shall be held, unless it be when our
churches, located in the same State, convene to
18 confer on a statute of said State, or to confer
harmoniously on individual unity and action of
the churches in said State.

21   **Titles.** SECT. 2.   "The First Church of
Christ, Scientist," is the legal title of The Mother

Church. Branch churches of The Mother Church   1
may take the title of First Church of Christ,
Scientist; Second Church of Christ, Scientist;   3
and so on, where more than one church is established in the same place; but the article
"The" must not be used before titles of branch   6
churches, nor written on applications for membership in naming such churches.

Mother Church Unique. SECT. 3. In its   9
relation to other Christian Science churches, in
its By-Laws and self-government, The Mother
Church stands alone; it occupies a position that   12
no other church can fill. Then for a branch
church to assume such position would be disas-
trous to Christian Science. Therefore, no Church   15
of Christ, Scientist, shall be considered loyal
that has branch churches or adopts The Mother
Church's form of government, except in such cases   18
as are specially allowed and named in this Manual.

Tenets Copyrighted. SECT. 4. Branch
churches shall not write the Tenets of The   21
Mother Church in their church books, except
they give the name of their author and her
permission to publish them as Tenets of The   24
Mother Church, copyrighted in SCIENCE AND
HEALTH WITH KEY TO THE SCRIPTURES.

1   **Manual.** Sect. 5. Branch churches shall
not adopt, print, nor publish the Manual of The
3 Mother Church. See Article XXXV, Sect. 1.

Organizing Churches. Sect. 6. A member
of this Church who obeys its By-Laws and is a
6 loyal exemplary Christian Scientist working in
the Field, is eligible to form a church in conformity with Sect. 7 of this Article, and to
9 have church services conducted by reading the
Scriptures and the Christian Science textbook.
This church shall be acknowledged publicly as a
12 Church of Christ, Scientist. Upon proper application, made in accordance with the rules of The
Christian Science Publishing Society, the serv-
15 ices of such a church may be advertised in *The
Christian Science Journal.* The branch churches
shall be individual, and not more than two small
18 churches shall consolidate under one church government. If the Pastor Emeritus, Mrs. Eddy,
should relinquish her place as the head or Leader
21 of The Mother Church of Christ, Scientist, each
branch church shall continue its present form of
government in consonance with The Mother
24 Church Manual.

**Requirements for Organizing Branch
Churches.** Sect. 7. A branch church of The
27 First Church of Christ, Scientist, Boston, Mass.,

shall not be organized with less than sixteen loyal   1
Christian Scientists, four of whom are members
of The Mother Church. This membership shall   3
include at least one active practitioner whose card
is published in the list of practitioners in *The*
Christian Science Journal.   6

Privilege of Members. SECT. 8. Members
in good standing with The Mother Church, who
are members of the faculty, instructors, or stu-.   9
dents in any university or college, can form and
conduct a Christian Science organization at such
university or college, provided its rules so permit.   12
Also members in good standing with The Mother
Church, who are graduates of said university
or college, may become members of the organ-   15
ization by application to, and by the unanimous
vote of, the active members present, if the rules
of the university or college so permit. When   18
called for, a member of the Board of Lectureship may lecture for said university or college
organization.   21

No Close Communion. SECT. 9. The
Mother Church and the branch churches shall
not confine their membership to the pupils of   24
one teacher.

No Interference. SECT. 10. A member of The
Mother Church may be a member of one branch   27

1 Church of Christ, Scientist, or of one Christian
Science society holding public services, but he
3 shall not be a member of both a branch church
and a society; neither shall he exercise super-
vision or control over any other church.   In
6 Christian Science each branch church shall be
distinctly democratic in its government, and no
individual, and no other church shall interfere
9 with its affairs.

Teachers' and Practitioners' Offices. SECT. 11.
Teachers and practitioners of Christian Science
12 shall not have their offices or rooms in the branch
churches, in the Reading Rooms, nor in rooms
connected therewith.

15 **Recognition.** SECT. 12. In order to be eligible to a card in *The Christian Science Journal*,
churches and societies are required to acknowl-
18 edge as such all other Christian Science churches
and societies advertised in said *Journal*, and to
maintain toward them an attitude of Christian
21 fellowship.

GUARDIANSHIP OF CHURCH FUNDS 1

Article XXIV

Church Edifice a Testimonial. Section 1. 3
Whereas, on March 20, 1895, the Christian Science Board of Directors, in behalf of The First Church of Christ, Scientist, Boston, Mass., 6 presented to Rev. Mary Baker Eddy their church edifice as a Testimonial of this Church's love and gratitude, and she, with grateful ac- 9 knowledgments thereof, declined to receive this munificent gift, she now understands the financial situation between the Christian Science 12 Board of Directors and said Church to be as follows: —

Financial Situation. Sect. 2. The Christian 15 Science Board of Directors owns the church edifices, with the land whereon they stand, legally; and the Church members own the aforesaid 18 premises and buildings, beneficially. After the first church was built, the balance of the building funds, which remained in the hands of the 21 Directors, belonged to the Church, and not solely to the Directors. The balance of the church

1 building funds, which can be spared after the
debts are paid, should remain on safe deposit,
3 to be hereafter used for the benefit of this
Church, as the right occasion may call for it.
The following indicates the proper management
6 of the Church funds: —

Report of Directors. SECT. 3. It shall be
the duty of the Christian Science Board of Di-
9 rectors to have the books of the Church Treasurer audited semi-annually, and to report at the
annual Church meeting the amount of funds
12 which the Church has on hand, the amount of
its indebtedness and of its expenditures for the
last year.

15 **Finance Committee.** SECT. 4. There shall
be a Committee on Finance, which shall consist of
three members of this Church in good standing.
18 Its members shall be appointed annually by the
Christian Science Board of Directors and with
the consent of the Pastor Emeritus. They shall
21 hold quarterly meetings and keep themselves
thoroughly informed as to the real estate owned
by this Church and the amount of funds received
24 by the Treasurer of The Mother Church, who is
individually responsible for said funds. They
shall have the books of the Christian Science

Board of Directors and the books of the Church
Treasurer audited annually by an honest, com-
petent accountant. The books are to be audited
on May first.

Prior to paying bills against the Church, the
Treasurer of this Church shall submit them all
to said committee for examination. This committee shall decide thereupon by a unanimous
vote, and its endorsement of the bills shall render
them payable.

If it be found that the Church funds have not
been properly managed, it shall be the duty of
the Board of Directors and the Treasurer to be
individually responsible for the performance of
their several offices satisfactorily, and for the
proper distribution of the funds of which they
are the custodians.

God's Requirement. Sect. 5. God requires
wisdom, economy, and brotherly love to char-
acterize all the proceedings of the members of
The Mother Church, The First Church of Christ,
Scientist.

Provision for the Future. Sect. 6. In case
of any possible future deviation from duty, the
Committee on Finance shall visit the Board of
Directors, and, in a Christian spirit and manner,

1 demand that each member thereof comply with
the By-Laws of the Church. If any Director
3 fails to heed this admonition, he may be dismissed from office and the vacancy supplied by
the Board.

6 **Debt and Duty.** Sect. 7. The Mother Church
shall not be made legally responsible for the debts
of individuals except such debts as are specified
9 in its By-Laws. Donations from this Church
shall not be made without the written consent
of the Pastor Emeritus. Also important move-
12 ments of the manager of the Committee on Publication shall be sanctioned by the Board of
Directors and be subject to the approval of Mary
15 Baker Eddy.   (See Article I, Sect. 6.)

  Emergencies. Sect. 8. The Treasurer, personally, or through the Clerk of the Church,
18 may pay from the funds of the Church bills of
immediate necessity not exceeding $200 for any
one transaction, and he may keep on deposit the
21 sum of $500 with the Clerk, as a petty cash
fund, to be used by him for the payment of
such bills. Such payments shall be reported, on
24 the first of the following month, to the Board
of Directors and the Committee on Finance, for
their approval.

Committee on Business. SECT. 9. The Christian Science Board of Directors shall elect annually a Committee on Business, which shall consist of not less than three loyal members of The Mother Church, who shall transact promptly and efficiently such business as Mrs. Eddy, the Directors, or the Committee on Publication shall commit to it. While the members of this Committee are engaged in the transaction of the business assigned to them they shall be paid from the Church funds. Before being eligible for office the names of the persons nominated for said office shall be presented to Mrs. Eddy for her written approval.

THE CHRISTIAN SCIENCE PUBLISHING SOCIETY

ARTICLE XXV

Board of Trustees. SECTION 1. The Board of Trustees, constituted by a Deed of Trust given by Rev. Mary Baker Eddy, the Pastor Emeritus of this Church, on January twenty-fifth, 1898, shall hold and manage the property therein conveyed, and conduct the business of

1 " The Christian Science Publishing Society " on
a strictly Christian basis, for the promotion of
3 the interests of Christian Science.

Disposal of Funds. SECT. 2. The net profits
of the business shall be paid over semi-annually
6 to the Treasurer of The Mother Church. He
shall hold this money subject to the order of
the Christian Science Board of Directors, which
9 is authorized to order its disposition only in
accordance with the By-Laws contained in this
Manual.

12 **Vacancies in Trusteeship.** SECT. 3. The
Christian Science Board of Directors shall have
the power to declare vacancies in said trusteeship,
15 for such reasons as to the Board may seem ex-
pedient.

Whenever a vacancy shall occur, the Pastor
18 Emeritus reserves the right to fill the same by
appointment; but if she does not elect to exercise this right, the remaining trustees shall fill
21 the vacancy, subject to her approval.

Editors and Manager. SECT. 4. The term
of office for the editors and the manager of The
24 Christian Science Publishing Society is one year
each, dating from the time of election to the
office. Incumbents who have served one year or

more can be re-elected, or new officers elected,   1
by a unanimous vote of the Christian Science
Board of Directors, and the consent of the Pastor   3
Emeritus given in her own handwriting.

Suitable Employees. Sect. 5. A person
who is not accepted by the Pastor Emeritus and   6
the Christian Science Board of Directors as
suitable, shall in no manner be connected with
publishing her books, nor with editing or pub-   9
lishing *The Christian Science Journal, Christian
Science Sentinel, Der Herold der Christian Science,* nor with The Christian Science Publishing   12
Society.

Periodicals. Sect. 6. Periodicals which
shall at any time be published by The Christian   15
Science Publishing Society, shall be copyrighted
and conducted according to the provisions in the
Deed of Trust relating to *The Christian Science*   18
Journal.

Rule of Conduct. Sect. 7. No objectionable
pictures shall be exhibited in the rooms where the   21
Christian Science textbook is published or sold.
No idle gossip, no slander, no mischief-making,
no evil speaking shall be allowed.   24

Books to be Published. Sect. 8. Only the
Publishing Society of The Mother Church selects,

6

approves, and publishes the books and literature it sends forth. If Mary Baker Eddy disap-
proves of certain books or literature, the Society
will not publish them. The Committees on Publication are in no manner connected with these
functions. A book or an article of which Mrs.
Eddy is the author shall not be published nor
republished by this Society without her knowledge or written consent.

Removal of Cards. SECT. 9. No cards shall
be removed from our periodicals without the request of the advertiser, except by a majority vote
of the Christian Science Board of Directors at
a meeting held for this purpose or for the examination of complaints.

Members of this Church who practise other
professions or pursue other vocations, shall not
advertise as healers, excepting those members
who are officially engaged in the work of Christian Science, and they must devote ample time
for faithful practice.

TEACHING CHRISTIAN SCIENCE

1

Article XXVI

TEACHERS

3

Motive in Teaching. SECTION 1. Teaching Christian Science shall not be a question of money, but of morals and religion, healing and 6 uplifting the race.

Care of Pupils. SECT. 2. Christian Scientists who are teachers shall carefully select for pupils 9 such only as have good past records and promising proclivities toward Christian Science. A teacher shall not assume personal control of, or 12 attempt to dominate his pupils, but he shall hold himself morally obligated to promote their progress in the understanding of divine Principle, not 15 only during the class term but after it, and to watch well that they prove sound in sentiment and practical in Christian Science. He shall per- 18 sistently and patiently counsel his pupils in conformity with the unerring laws of God, and shall enjoin them habitually to study the Scriptures 21 and SCIENCE AND HEALTH WITH KEY TO THE SCRIPTURES as a help thereto.

1 **Defense against Malpractice.** SECT. 3.
Teachers shall instruct their pupils how to de-
3 fend themselves against mental malpractice,
never to return evil for evil, but to know the
truth that makes free, and thus to be a law, not
6 unto others, but to themselves.

Number of Pupils. SECT. 4. The teachers of
Christian Science shall teach but one class yearly,
9 which class shall consist of not more than thirty
pupils. After 1907, the Board of Education shall
have one class triennially, a Normal class not
12 exceeding thirty pupils.

Pupil's Tuition. SECT. 5. A student's price
for teaching Christian Science shall not exceed
15 $100.00 per pupil.

Associations. SECT. 6. The associations of the
pupils of loyal teachers shall convene annually.
18 The pupils shall be guided by the BIBLE, and
SCIENCE AND HEALTH, not by their teachers'
personal views. Teachers shall not call their
21 pupils together, or assemble a selected number of
them, for more frequent meetings.

A Single Field of Labor. SECT. 7. A loyal
24 teacher of Christian Science shall not teach another loyal teacher's pupil, except it be in the
Board of Education. Outside of this Board each

student occupies only his own field of labor.
Pupils may visit each other's churches, and by
invitation attend each other's associations.

Caring for Pupils of Strayed Members.
SECT. 8. A loyal teacher of Christian Science
may teach and receive into his association the
pupils of another member of this Church who
has so strayed as justly to be deemed, under the
provisions of Article XII, Sect. 1, not ready to
lead his pupils.

Teachers must have Certificates. SECT. 9.
A member of this Church shall not teach pupils
Christian Science unless he has a certificate to
show that he has been taught by Mrs. Eddy or
has taken a Normal Course at the Massachusetts Metaphysical College or in the Board of
Education.

Such members who have not been continu-
ously active and loyal Christian Scientists since
receiving instruction as above, shall not teach
Christian Science without the approval of the
Christian Science Board of Directors.

Article XXVII

PUPILS

Authorized to Teach. Section 1. After a student's pupil has been duly authorized to be a teacher of Christian Science, or has been under the personal instruction of Mrs. Eddy, he is no longer under the jurisdiction of his former teacher.

Without Teachers. Sect. 2. Those beloved brethren whose teacher has left them, can elect an experienced Christian Scientist, who is not in charge of an association of students and who is ready for this high calling, to conduct the meetings of their association.

Basis for Teaching. Sect. 3. The teachers of the Normal class shall teach from the chapter " Recapitulation " in Science and Health with Key to the Scriptures, and from the Christian Science Platform, beginning on page 330 of the revised editions since 1902, and they shall teach nothing contrary thereto. The teachers of the Primary class shall instruct their pupils from the said chapter on " Recapitulation " only.

Church Membership. SECT. 4. Neither the
Pastor Emeritus nor a member of this Church
shall teach Roman Catholics Christian Science,
except it be with the written consent of the
authority of their Church. Choice of patients is
left to the wisdom of the practitioner, and Mrs.
Eddy is not to be consulted on this subject.

Class Teaching. SECT. 5. Members of The
Mother Church who are authorized by its By-
Laws to teach Christian Science, shall not solicit,
or cause or permit others to solicit, pupils for their
classes. No member of this Church shall advise
against class instruction.

Teachers of Christian Science must have the
necessary moral and spiritual qualifications to
elucidate the Principle and rule of Christian Science, through the higher meaning of the Scriptures. " The less the teacher personally controls
other minds, and the more he trusts them to the
divine Truth and Love, the better it will be for
both teacher and student." (Retrospection and
Introspection, page 84.)

BOARD OF EDUCATION

Article XXVIII

ORGANIZATION

Officers. Section 1. There shall be a Board of Education, under the auspices of Mary Baker Eddy, President of the Massachusetts Metaphysical College, consisting of three members, a president, vice-president, and teacher of Christian Science. Obstetrics will not be taught.

Election. Sect. 2. The vice-president shall be elected annually by the Christian Science Board of Directors. Beginning with 1907, the teacher shall be elected every third year by said Board, and the candidate shall be subject to the approval of the Pastor Emeritus.

President not to be Consulted. Sect. 3. The President is not to be consulted by students on the question of applying for admission to this Board nor on their course or conduct. The students can confer with their teachers on subjects essential to their progress.

Presidency of College. Sect. 4. Should the 1
President resign over her own signature or va-
cate her office of President of the Massachusetts 3
Metaphysical College, a meeting of the Christian
Science Board of Directors shall immediately be
called, and the vice-president of the Board of 6
Education being found worthy, on receiving her
approval shall be elected to fill the vacancy.

Article XXIX 9

APPLICANTS AND GRADUATES

Normal Teachers. Section 1. Loyal students who have been taught in a Primary class 12
by Mrs. Eddy and have practised Christian Science healing acceptably three years, and who present such credentials as are required to verify 15
this fact, are eligible to receive the degree of
C. S. D.

Qualifications. Sect. 2. Loyal Christian 18
Scientists' pupils who so desire may apply to the
Board of Education for instruction; and if they
have practised Christian Science healing success- 21
fully three years and will furnish evidence of
their eligibility therefor, they are eligible to enter

1 the Normal class. All members of this class must
be thorough English scholars.

3 **Certificates.** Sect. 3. Students are examined
and given certificates by this Board if found
qualified to receive them.

6 ARTICLE XXX

ACTION OF THE BOARD

Sessions. Section 1. The term of the
9 Massachusetts Metaphysical College will open
with the Board of Education on the first
Wednesday of December. The sessions will
12 continue not over one week. None but the
teacher and members of the College class shall
be present at the sessions, and no Primary
15 classes shall be taught under the auspices of
this Board.

Special Instruction. Sect. 2. Not less than
18 two thorough lessons by a well qualified teacher
shall be given to each Normal class on the
subject of mental practice and *malpractice*. One
21 student in the class shall prepare a paper on
said subject that shall be read to the class,
thoroughly discussed, and understood; this paper

shall be given to the teacher, and he shall not allow it or a copy of it to remain, but shall destroy this paper.

Signatures. Sect. 3. The signature of the teacher and of the President of the College shall be on all certificates issued.

Remuneration and Free Scholarship. Sect. 4. Tuition of class instruction in the Board of Education shall be $100.00. The bearer of a card of free scholarship from the President, Rev. Mary Baker Eddy, shall be entitled to a free course in this department on presentation of the card to the teacher. Only the President gives free admission to classes.

Surplus Funds. Sect. 5. Any surplus funds left in the hands of the Board of Education shall be paid over annually to the Treasurer of The Mother Church.

Primary Students. Sect. 6. Students of Christian Science, duly instructed therein and with good moral records, not having the certificate of C. S. D. may enter the Normal class in the Board of Education, which will be held once in three years beginning A. D. **1907;** provided their diplomas are for three *consecutive* years under Mrs. Eddy's daily conversation on Chris-

1 tian Science, or from the Massachusetts Metaphysical College Board of Education.

3 **Healing Better than Teaching.** SECT. 7.
Healing the sick and the sinner with Truth dem-
onstrates what we affirm of Christian Science,
6 and nothing can substitute this demonstration.
I recommend that each member of this Church
shall strive to demonstrate by his or her practice,
9 that Christian Science heals the sick quickly and
wholly, thus proving this Science to be all that
we claim for it.

12   If both husband and wife are found duly qualified to teach Christian Science, either one, not
both, should teach yearly one class.

15 **Not Members of The Mother Church.** SECT. 8.
No person shall receive instructions in Christian Science in any class in the Massachusetts
18 Metaphysical College, nor receive the degree of
C. S. B. or C. S. D., who is not a member of The
First Church of Christ, Scientist, in Boston,
21 Mass.

Only those persons who are members of this
Church and possessed of the qualifications named
24 in Sect. 9 of Article XXVI of these By-Laws
shall be deemed loyal teachers of Christian
Science.

BOARD OF LECTURESHIP

ARTICLE XXXI

ORGANIZATION AND DUTIES

Election. SECTION 1. This Church shall maintain a Board of Lectureship, the members of which shall be elected annually on Monday preceding the Annual Meeting, subject to the approval of the Pastor Emeritus. The lecture year shall begin July 1 of each year.

Duty of Lecturers. SECT. 2. It is the duty of the Board of Lectureship to include in each lecture a true and just reply to public topics condemning Christian Science, and to bear testimony to the facts pertaining to the life of the Pastor Emeritus. Each member shall mail to the Clerk of this Church copies of his lectures before delivering them.

No Disruption of Branch Churches. SECT. 3. The Board of Lectureship is not allowed in anywise to meddle with nor to disrupt the organiza-

1 tion of branch churches. The lecturer can invite
churches within the city whither he is called to
3 unite in their attendance on his lecture, and so
make for their churches a less lecture fee; but
the churches shall decide their action.

6 **Receptions.** SECT. 4. As a rule there should
be no receptions nor festivities after a lecture on
Christian Science, but there may occur excep-
9 tions. If there be an individual who goes to hear
and deride truth, he should go away contemplat-
ing truth; and he who goes to seek truth should
12 have the opportunity to depart in quiet *thought*
on that subject.

Circuit Lecturer. SECT. 5. Upon the written
15 request of Mrs. Eddy, The Mother Church shall
appoint a Circuit Lecturer. His term of office, if
approved, shall not be less than three years. He
18 shall lecture in the United States, in Canada, in
Great Britain and Ireland.

A member shall neither resign nor transfer
21 this sacred office.

Article XXXII

CALLS FOR LECTURES

From the Directors. Section 1. When the need is apparent, the Christian Science Board of Directors of The Mother Church may call on any member of this Board of Lectureship to lecture at such places and at such times as the cause of Christian Science demands.

From Branch Churches. Sect. 2. The branch Churches of Christ, Scientist, may apply through their clerks to a member of this Board of Lectureship for a speaker, and one shall be assigned them by the Board.

From Societies. Sect. 3. If called for, a member of the Board may lecture for a Society.

Annual Lectures. Sect. 4. The Mother Church and the branch churches shall call on the Board of Lectureship annually for one or more lectures.

No Lectures by Readers. Sect. 5. No lecture shall be given by a Reader during his term of Readership. The duties alone of a Reader are ample.

1   **No Wednesday Evening Lectures.** SECT. 6. The Board of Lectureship shall not appoint a
3 lecture for Wednesday evening.

    Lecture Fee. SECT. 7. The lecture fee shall be left to the discretion of the lecturer.

6   **Expenses.** SECT. 8. The lecturer's traveling expenses and the cost of hall shall be paid by the church that employs him.

9   **Exceptional Cases.** SECT. 9. If a lecturer receive a call to lecture in a place where he sees there is special need, and the local church is un-
12 able to meet the expense, he is at liberty to supply that need and trust to contributions for his fee.

COMMITTEE ON PUBLICATION 1

Article XXXIII

In The Mother Church. Section 1. There 3
shall be appointed by The Mother Church a Committee on Publication, which shall consist of one
loyal Christian Scientist who lives in Boston, and 6
he shall be manager of the Committees on Publication throughout the United States, Canada,
Great Britain and Ireland. He shall be elected 9
annually by a unanimous vote of the Christian
Science Board of Directors and the consent of
the Pastor Emeritus given in her own handwrit- 12
ing, and shall receive an annual salary, paid quarterly, of not less than four thousand dollars.

Duties. Sect. 2. It shall be the duty of the 15
Committee on Publication to correct in a Christian manner impositions on the public in regard
to Christian Science, injustices done Mrs. Eddy 18
or members of this Church by the daily press,
by periodicals or circulated literature of any sort.

7

1 This Committee on Publication shall be responsible for correcting or having corrected a false
3 newspaper article which has not been replied to
by other Scientists, or which has been forwarded
to this Committee for the purpose of having him
6 reply to it. If the correction by the Committee
on Publication is not promptly published by the
periodical in which it is desirable that this cor-
9 rection shall appear, this Committee shall immediately apply for aid to the Committee on
Business. Furthermore, the Committee on Pub-
12 lication shall read the *last proof sheet* of such
an article and see that it is published according
to copy; he shall circulate in large quantities
15 the papers containing such an article, sending a
copy to the Clerk of the Church. It shall also
be the duty of the Committee on Publication to
18 have published each year in a leading Boston
newspaper the letter sent to the Pastor Emeritus
by the Church members in annual meeting as-
21 sembled. The State Committees on Publication
act under the direction of this Committee on
Publication.

24   **In Branch Churches.** SECT. 3. The Readers
of the three largest branch churches in each State
of the United States and in Canada shall annually

and alternately appoint a Committee on Publication to serve in their localities. For the purposes of this By-Law, the State of California shall
be considered as though it were two States, the
dividing line being the 36th parallel of latitude.
Each county of Great Britain and Ireland, except
as hereinafter specified, through the Readers of
its three largest branch churches, shall annually
and alternately appoint a Committee on Publication to serve in its locality. Each church is not
necessarily confined to its own members in select-
ing this Committee, but if preferred, can appoint
a Committee on Publication who is in good fellowship with another Church of Christ, Scientist.

This By-Law applies to all States except Massachusetts, in which the Committee on Publication is elected only by the Christian Science Board
of Directors. The Committee for the counties
in which London, England, is situated shall be
appointed by the Christian Science Board of
Directors, and he shall, in addition to his other
duties, act as District Manager of the Committees
on Publication for Great Britain and Ireland.

Appointment. Sect. 4. The Committees on
Publication shall consist of men generally. Each
State Committee shall be appointed by the First
and Second Readers of the church employing

1 said Committee. If prior to the meeting of the
church for the election of officers, Mrs. Eddy
3 shall send to the First Reader of the church the
name of a candidate for its Committee on Publication, the Readers shall appoint said candidate.
6 Or if she shall send a special request to any
Committee on Publication, the request shall be
carried out according to her directions.

9 **Removal from Office.** SECT. 5. If the Committee on Publication neglects to fulfil the obligations of his office according to these By-Laws,
12 and this becomes apparent to the Christian Science Board of Directors, it shall be the duty of
the Directors immediately to act upon this im-
15 portant matter in accordance with said By-Laws.

The Christian Science Board of Directors may
notify any Church of Christ, Scientist, to remove
18 its Committee on Publication and to appoint another Committee to fill the vacancy; and it shall
be the duty of that church to comply with this
21 request. In such cases it shall be the privilege
of this Board to name the Committee if it so
desires, and any Committee so named by the
24 Board shall be elected by the branch church.

Case of Necessity. SECT. 6. If a suitable
man is not obtainable for Committee on Publica-
27 tion, a suitable woman shall be elected. If at

any time the Christian Science Board of Direc- 1
tors shall determine that the manager of the
general Committee on Publication needs an as- 3
sistant, the Board shall, with the approval of the
Pastor Emeritus, appoint an assistant manager,
who shall receive an adequate salary from The 6
Mother Church.

CHURCH–BUILDING

ARTICLE XXXIV

Building Committee. SECTION 1.   There
shall be a Building Committee consisting of
not less than three members, and this committee
shall not be dissolved until the new church
edifice is completed.   This committee shall elect,
dismiss, or supply a vacancy of its members by
a majority vote.

Designation of Deeds. SECT. 2.   All deeds
of further purchases of land for The First
Church of Christ, Scientist, in Boston, Mass.,
shall have named in them all the trusts mentioned
in the deeds given by Albert Metcalf and E.
Noyes Whitcomb in March, 1903; but this rule
shall not apply to land purchased for any purpose
other than the erection of a church edifice.   Also
there shall be incorporated in all such deeds
the phrase, " Mary Baker Eddy's Church, The

Mother Church or The First Church of Christ, 1
Scientist, in Boston, Mass."

The Mother Church Building. SECT. 3. The 3
edifice erected in 1894 for The First Church of
Christ, Scientist, in Boston, Mass., shall neither
be demolished, nor removed from the site where 6
it was built, without the written consent of the
Pastor Emeritus, Mary Baker Eddy.

CHURCH MANUAL

Article XXXV

For The Mother Church Only. Section 1. The Church Manual of The First Church of Christ, Scientist, in Boston, Mass., written by Mary Baker Eddy and copyrighted, is adapted to The Mother Church only. It stands alone, uniquely adapted to form the budding thought and hedge it about with divine Love. This Manual shall not be revised without the written consent of its author.

Seventy-third Edition the Authority. Sect. 2. The Board of Directors, the Committee on Bible Lessons, and the Board of Trustees shall each keep a copy of the Seventy-third Edition and of subsequent editions of the Church Manual; and if a discrepancy appears in any revised edition, these editions shall be cited as authority.

Amendment of By-Laws. SECT. 3. No new
Tenet or By-Law shall be adopted, nor any
Tenet or By-Law amended or annulled, without the written consent of Mary Baker Eddy, the
author of our textbook, SCIENCE AND HEALTH.

Appendix

Appendix

Special Instructions

Regarding Applications for Church Membership

1. Loyal members of The Mother Church are eligible to approve candidates to unite with this Church.

2. No persons are eligible to countersign applications except loyal students of Mrs. Eddy, Directors, and students of the Board of Education who have been given a degree, and are members of The Mother Church.

3. Those who approve applicants should have applications returned to them after being filled out by the applicants, as required by Article V, Sect. 6, and should compare them with the forms here given, and see that names are legibly written, before sending them to the Clerk of the Church. If not correct, the applicant will be notified, and new applications will

1 be required, as none will be returned that are
not correctly made out. This requirement is to
3 prevent applications being duplicated and the
confusion that might result therefrom. It is
important that these seemingly strict conditions
6 be exactly complied with, as the names of the
members of The Mother Church will be recorded
in the history of the Church and become a part
9 thereof.

4. All names, whether of applicants, ap-
provers, or countersigners, must be plainly
12 written, and one, at least, of the given names of
each, written in full. Initials only of first names
will not be received. Women must sign " Miss "
15 or " Mrs." before their names as the case may be.

All names must be written the same in all
places where they are required.

TO APPLICANTS   1

1. In filling out the application blank, one of the Christian names must be written in full. 3 Initials alone will not be received.

2. If the applicant is a married woman she must sign her own Christian name, not her hus- 6 band's, and prefix her signature with " Mrs; " unmarried women must sign " Miss."

3. There are two regular forms of applica- 9 tion. 1. For those who have studied Christian Science with an authorized teacher; 2. For those who have not studied Christian Science with a 12 teacher.

Applicants will find the chief points of these instructions illustrated in Form 1 and Form 2, 15 on pages 114 and 118.

4. Those whose teachers are deceased, absent, or disloyal, or those whose teachers refuse, with- 18 out sufficient cause, to sign applications (see Art. V, Sect. 4), will be furnished special forms on application to the Clerk.   21

1   5. When branch churches are designated by number, as First Church, Second Church, etc.,
3 the number must be written First, Second, as shown on page 118. The article " the " either capitalized (The), or small (the), must not be
6 used before titles of branch churches. See Article XXIII, Sect. 2.

   6. If the applicant is not a member of a
9 branch church, he should fill out his application in this respect according to the form on page 114.

Application Forms

APPLICATION

I

PROPERLY SIGNED AND ENDORSED, ACCORD-
ING TO ARTICLE V, SECT. 2

FORM 1.

The First Church of Christ, Scientist, in Boston, Mass., is designed to be built on the rock of Christ — Truth and Life — and to reflect the Church Triumphant.

One who is not a member of any church, excepting a branch church of Christ, Scientist, who loves Christian Science, and reads understandingly the Bible, and SCIENCE AND HEALTH WITH KEY TO THE SCRIPTURES, by Reverend Mary Baker Eddy, and other works by this author, and who is Christianly qualified and can enter into full fellowship with the Tenets and Rules of The First Church of Christ, Scientist, in Boston, Mass., is eligible to membership.

To The First Church of Christ, Scientist, in Boston, Mass.

Ezra W. Palmer, Clerk.

I hereby make application for membership, and subscribe to the Tenets and the By-Laws of the Church.

My teacher in Christian Science is

.....................*James B. Brown, C.S.D.*...................

I am not a member of any church.

If you have been taught by a loyal student who has taken a degree at the Massachusetts Metaphysical College, or by one who has passed an examination by the Board of Education, fill this blank.

APPLICATION

I — (*Continued*)

PROPERLY SIGNED AND ENDORSED, ACCORDING TO ARTICLE V, SECT. 2

FORM 1, — (*Continued.*)

I was formerly a member of the ....
.... denomination,
but have definitely severed my connection therewith.

Name............*Mrs. Jennie W. Field, C.S.*...........

Street and Number.........*18 Forest St.,*....................

Town or City..............................*Chicago,*..........

State...*Ill*........

Date..............*Jan. 2nd, 1901.*...........................

I cordially approve the applicant.

(*a*)...................*James B. Brown, C.S.D.*...............

Countersigned by...

DO NOT DETACH.

To the Applicant:

Please fill out the following for the use of the Treasurer of the Church :

Name..... *Mrs. Jennie W. Field, C.S.,*.........

Street and Number....*18 Forest St.,*...........

Town or City..........................*Chicago,*.........

State..*Ill.*

APPLICATION

I

PROPERLY SIGNED AND ENDORSED, ACCORDING TO ARTICLE V, SECT. 2

FORM 1.

The First Church of Christ, Scientist, in Boston, Mass., is designed to be built on the rock of Christ — Truth and Life — and to reflect the Church Triumphant.

One who is not a member of any church, excepting a branch church of Christ, Scientist, who loves Christian Science, and reads understandingly the Bible, and SCIENCE AND HEALTH WITH KEY TO THE SCRIPTURES, by Reverend Mary Baker Eddy, and other works by this author, and who is Christianly qualified and can enter into full fellowship with the Tenets and Rules of The First Church of Christ, Scientist, in Boston, Mass., is eligible to membership.

To The First Church of Christ, Scientist, in Boston, Mass.

Ezra W. Palmer, Clerk.

I hereby make application for membership, and subscribe to the Tenets and the By-Laws of the Church.

My teacher in Christian Science is

...................*James B. Brown, C.S.D.*...................

I am not a member of any church, ~~excepting~~...................
~~Church of Christ, Scientist, at~~...................

APPLICATION

I — (*Continued*)

PROPERLY SIGNED AND ENDORSED, ACCORDING TO ARTICLE V, SECT. 2

FORM 1, — (*Continued.*)

I was formerly a member of the ....
.... denomination,
but have definitely severed my connection therewith.

Name............*Mrs. Jennie W. Field, C.S.*............

Street and Number............*Forest St.,*..................

Town or City..................................*Chicago,*..................

State..*Ill*............

Date............*Jan. 2nd, 1901.*..................................

I cordially approve this **applicant.**

(*a*)................*James B. Brown, C.S.D.*................

Countersigned by..

DO NOT DETACH.

To the Applicant:

Please fill out the following for the use of the Treasurer of the Church :

Name..... *Mrs. Jennie W. Field, C.S.,*........

Street and Number........*Forest St.,*............

Town or City.....................*Chicago,*........

State...*Ill.*

APPLICATION

II

SIGNED, ENDORSED, AND COUNTERSIGNED, ACCORDING TO ARTICLE VI, SECT. 2

If you have not been taught by a loyal student who has taken a degree at the Massachusetts Metaphysical College, or by one who has passed an examination by the Board of Education, fill this blank.

FORM 2.

One who is not a member of any church, excepting a branch church of Christ, Scientist, who loves Christian Science, and reads understandingly the Bible, and SCIENCE AND HEALTH WITH KEY TO THE SCRIPTURES, by Reverend Mary Baker Eddy, and other works by this author, and who is Christianly qualified and can enter into full fellowship with the Tenets and Rules of The First Church of Christ, Scientist, in Boston, Mass., is eligible to membership.

To The First Church of Christ, Scientist, in Boston, Mass.

Ezra W. Palmer, Clerk.

I hereby make application for membership, and subscribe to the Tenets and the By-Laws of the Church. I have not studied Christian Science with a teacher, and am not a member of any church excepting *Second* Church of Christ, Scientist, at *New York, N. Y.*

I was formerly a member of the................................
.... denomination, but have definitely severed my connection therewith.

APPLICATION
II — (*Continued*)

SIGNED, ENDORSED, AND COUNTERSIGNED,
ACCORDING TO ARTICLE VI, SECT. 2

FORM 2, — (*Continued.*)

Name............*Miss Emma L. French*..................

Street and Number..........*293 Emerson St.,*..........

Town or City.............................*New York*..........

State...*N. Y.*......

Date...............*Jan. 2nd, 1901.*..........................

I cordially approve this applicant.

(*a*)................*Miss Mary E. Grant, C.S.*............

Countersigned by........*James B. Brown, C.S.D.*......

DO NOT DETACH.

Name.......*Miss Emma L. French*..............

To the Applicant:

Please fill out the Street and Number..... *293 Emerson St.*......
following for the use
of the Treasurer of Town or City......................*New York*.....
the Church:

State..*N. Y.*

Present Order of Services in The Mother Church and Branch Churches

Republished from the Sentinel

SUNDAY SERVICES

---

1. Hymn.
2. Reading a Scriptural Selection.
3. Silent Prayer, followed by the audible repetition of the Lord's Prayer with its spiritual interpretation.
4. Hymn.
5. Announcing necessary notices.
6. Solo.
7. Reading the Explanatory Note on first leaf of *Quarterly*.
8. Announcing the subject of the Lesson-Sermon, and reading the Golden Text.
9. Reading the Scriptural Selection, entitled "Responsive Reading," alternately by the First Reader and the congregation.
10. Reading the Lesson-Sermon. (After the Second Reader reads the BIBLE references of

the first Section of the Lesson, the First Reader makes the following announcement: " As announced in the explanatory note, I shall now read correlative passages from the Christian Science textbook, SCIENCE AND HEALTH WITH KEY TO THE SCRIPTURES, by Mary Baker Eddy.")

11.   Collection.

12.   Hymn.

13.   Reading the Scientific Statement of Being, and the correlative SCRIPTURE according to I John 3:1–3.

14.   Pronouncing Benediction.

The services should be preceded and followed by organ or piano music of an appropriate character in all cases where this is possible.

On the first Sunday of each month Article VIII, SECT. 1, *A Rule for Motives and Acts*, is to be read.

WEDNESDAY MEETINGS

1.   Hymn.

2.   Reading from the BIBLE, and correlative passages from SCIENCE AND HEALTH WITH KEY TO THE SCRIPTURES.

3.   Silent Prayer, followed by the audible repetition of the Lord's Prayer, its spiritual interpretation being omitted.

4.   Hymn.

5.   Announcing necessary notices.

6.   Experiences, testimonies, and remarks on Christian Science.

7.   Closing Hymn.

The services should be preceded and followed by organ or piano music of an appropriate character in all cases where this is possible.

Thanksgiving Day

*Order of Service for The Mother Church and
Branch Churches*

---

1. Hymn.

2. Reading the Thanksgiving Proclamation of the President of the United States, or the Governor of the state, or both.

3. Reading a Scriptural Selection.

4. Silent Prayer, followed by the audible repetition of the Lord's Prayer with its spiritual interpretation.

5. Hymn.

6. Reading the Explanatory Note on the first leaf of the *Quarterly*.

7. Announcing the subject of the Lesson-Sermon, and reading the Golden Text.

8. Responsive Reading by the First Reader and the congregation.

9.   Reading the Lesson-Sermon prepared by the Bible Lesson Committee.

10.   Solo.

11.   Testimonies by Christian Scientists, appropriate for the occasion.

12.   Hymn.

13.   Reading the Scientific Statement of Being, and the correlative SCRIPTURE according to I John 3:1–3.

14.   Pronouncing Benediction.

No collection is to be taken at this service.

The services should be preceded and followed by organ or piano music of an appropriate character in all cases where this is possible.

Present Order of Communion Services in Branch Churches

1.   Hymn.

2.   Reading a Scriptural Selection.

3.   Silent Prayer, followed by the audible repetition of the Lord's Prayer with its spiritual interpretation.

4.   Hymn.

5.   Announcing necessary notices.

6.   Reading Tenets of The Mother Church.

7.   Collection and Solo.

8.   Reading the Explanatory Note on first leaf of *Quarterly*.

9.   Announcing the subject of the Lesson-Sermon, and reading the Golden Text.

10.   Reading the Scriptural Selection entitled " Responsive Reading " alternately by the First Reader and the congregation.

11.   Reading the Lesson-Sermon.   (After the Second Reader reads the BIBLE references of the first Section of the Lesson, the First Reader

makes the following announcement: " As announced in the explanatory note, I shall now read correlative passages from the Christian Science textbook, SCIENCE AND HEALTH WITH KEY TO THE SCRIPTURES, by Mary Baker Eddy.")

12. The First Reader briefly invites the congregation to kneel in silent Communion. This is concluded by the audible repetition of the Lord's Prayer (spiritual interpretation omitted).

13. Singing the Doxology:

> " Be Thou, O God, exalted high;
> And as Thy glory fills the sky,
> So let it be on earth displayed,
> Till Thou art here and now obeyed."

14. Reading the Scientific Statement of Being and the correlative SCRIPTURE according to I John 3:1–3.

15. Pronouncing Benediction.

The Church Tenets shall be read at this service.

The services should be preceded and followed by organ or piano music of an appropriate character in all cases where this is possible.

Order of Exercises for the Sunday School of The Mother Church and Branch Churches [1]

1. Call to order by the Superintendent.

2. Hymn.

3. Subject of the lesson announced; Golden Text repeated by the children; Responsive Reading.

4. Silent prayer, followed by the audible repetition of the Lord's Prayer in unison.

5. Instruction in classes, in accordance with Sections 2 and 3 of Article XX of the Manual of The Mother Church.

6. Entire school reassembles.

7. Hymn.

8. Scientific Statement of Being read by the Superintendent.

9. School dismissed.

---

1 If a collection is taken, it should be taken in the classes before they reassemble.

Deed of Trust

*The following is a Copy of the Deed of Trust
Conveying Land for Church Edifice*

KNOW ALL MEN BY THESE PRESENTS,

That I Mary Baker G. Eddy of Concord in
the County of Merrimack and State of New
Hampshire in consideration of one dollar to
me paid by Ira O. Knapp of Boston, Massachusetts, William B. Johnson of Boston,
Massachusetts, Joseph S. Eastaman of Chel-
sea, Massachusetts, and Stephen A. Chase of
Fall River, Massachusetts, the receipt whereof
is hereby acknowledged, and, also in consideration of the trusts and uses hereinafter mentioned and established, do hereby give, bargain,
sell, and convey to the said Ira O. Knapp, William B. Johnson, Joseph S. Eastaman, and
Stephen A. Chase as trustees as hereinafter
provided and to their legitimate successors in

office forever, a certain parcel of land situate
on Falmouth street in said Boston, bounded and
described as follows: Beginning at the junction
of Falmouth street, and a forty-foot street now
called Caledonia street; thence running South-
west on said Falmouth street one hundred and
sixteen and eighty-eight hundredths feet; thence
Northwest at a right angle to a point where a
line drawn at right angles to said forty-foot
street at a point thereon one hundred and sixteen and fifty-five hundredths feet Northwest
from the point of beginning meets the said
boundary at right angles to Falmouth street,
sixty-six and seventy-eight hundredths feet;
thence at an obtuse angle on said line at right
angles to said forty-foot street sixty-seven and
thirty-five hundredths feet to said forty-foot
street; thence Southeasterly on said forty-foot
street one hundred and sixteen and fifty-five
hundredths feet to the point of beginning;
containing seven thousand eight hundred and
twenty-eight square feet more or less, and subject to the agreements and restrictions mentioned in a deed recorded in Suffolk Registry
of Deeds Lib. 1719, Fol. 83 so far as the same
are now legally operative.

9

This deed of conveyance is made upon the following express trusts and conditions which the said grantees by accepting this deed agree and covenant for themselves and their successors in office to fully perform and fulfil.

1. Said grantees shall be known as the " Christian Science Board of Directors," and shall constitute a perpetual body or corporation under and in accordance with section one, Chapter 39 of the Public Statutes of Massachusetts.[1] Whenever a vacancy occurs in said Board the remaining members shall within thirty days fill the same by election; but no one shall be eligible to that office who is not in the opinion of the remaining members of the Board a firm and consistent believer in the doctrines of Christian Science as taught in a book entitled " SCIENCE AND HEALTH," by Mary Baker G. Eddy beginning with the seventy-first edition thereof.

---

[1] The deacons, church wardens, or other similar officers of churches or other religious societies, and the trustees of the Methodist Episcopal churches appointed according to the discipline and usages thereof, shall, if citizens of this commonwealth, be deemed bodies corporate for the purpose of taking and holding in succession all the grants and donations, whether of real or personal estate, made either to them and their successors, or to their respective churches, or to the poor of the churches.

2. Said Board shall within five years from the date hereof build or cause to be built upon said lot of land a suitable and convenient church edifice, the cost of which shall not be less than fifty thousand dollars.

3. When said church building is completed said Board shall elect a pastor, reader or speaker to fill the pulpit who shall be a genuine Christian Scientist; they shall maintain public worship in accordance with the doctrines of Christian Science in said church, and for this purpose they are fully empowered to make any and all necessary rules and regulations.

4. Said Board of Directors shall not suffer or allow any building to be erected upon said lot except a church building or edifice, nor shall they allow said church building or any part thereof to be used for any other purpose than for the ordinary and usual uses of a church.

5. Said Board of Directors shall not allow or permit in said church building any preaching or other religious services which shall not be consonant and in strict harmony with the doctrines and practice of Christian Science as taught and explained by Mary Baker G. Eddy in the seventy-

first edition of her book entitled " SCIENCE AND
HEALTH," which is soon to be issued, and in any
subsequent edition thereof.

6.   The congregation which shall worship in
said church shall be styled " The First Church
of Christ, Scientist."

7.   Said Directors shall not sell or mortgage
the land hereby conveyed; but they shall see
that all taxes and legal assessments on said
property are promptly paid.

8.   Said church building shall not be removed
from said lot except for the purpose of rebuild-
ing thereon a more expensive or a more convenient structure in which said doctrines of Christian
Science only shall be preached and practised. If
said church building is removed for either of
the purposes above set forth, any and all tablets
and inscriptions which are or shall be upon said
church building at the time of removal shall be
removed therefrom and placed upon the walls
of the new edifice. If said building is burned,
the Directors shall forthwith proceed to rebuild
the church.

9.   Said Directors shall maintain regular
preaching, reading or speaking in said church

on each Sabbath, and an omission to have and maintain such preaching, reading or speaking for one year in succession shall be deemed a breach of this condition.

10.   Whenever said Directors shall determine that it is inexpedient to maintain preaching, reading or speaking in said church in accordance with the terms of this deed, they are authorized and required to reconvey forthwith said lot of land with the building thereon to Mary Baker G. Eddy, her heirs and assigns forever by a proper deed of conveyance.

11.   The omission or neglect on the part of said Directors to strictly comply with any of the conditions herein contained shall constitute a breach thereof, and the title hereby conveyed shall revert to the grantor Mary Baker G. Eddy, her heirs and assigns forever, upon her entry upon said land and taking possession thereof for such breach.

To Have and to Hold the above granted premises with all the privileges and appurtenances thereon belonging to said grantees and their successors in office to the uses and trusts above described forever.

And the said grantor for herself and her heirs, executors and administrators covenants with the said grantees and their successors in office that she is lawfully seized in fee simple of the aforesaid premises, that they are free from all incumbrances not herein mentioned or referred to, that she has good right to sell and convey the same to the said grantees and their successors in office as aforesaid, and that she will and her heirs, executors, and administrators shall, warrant and defend the same to the said grantees and their successors in office forever against the lawful claims and demands of all persons.

In witness whereof I the said Mary Baker G. Eddy have hereto set my hand and seal this 1st day of September, 1892.

MARY BAKER G. EDDY.

Signed, sealed, and delivered in presence of

LAURA E. SARGENT.

R. E. WALKER.

September 1st, 1892.

STATE OF NEW HAMPSHIRE, } ss.
    MERRIMACK.

Then personally appeared the above named Mary Baker G. Eddy and acknowledged the foregoing instrument to be her free act and deed,

Before me

R. E. WALKER.

Notary Public.

September 2, 1892.

SUFFOLK REGISTRY OF DEEDS, Lib. 2081, Fol. 257.

Deed Conveying Land for
Church Purposes

METCALF *to* KNAPP *et al. Trs.*
Libro 2886, Fol. 521.

KNOW ALL MEN,

That I, Albert Metcalf, the grantor in a certain deed given to Ira O. Knapp and others dated October 23, 1896, and recorded with Suffolk Deeds, Book 2591, page 398, do hereby declare that the land conveyed by said deed was conveyed to the grantees therein, as they are the Christian Science Board of Directors, upon the trusts, but not subject to the conditions mentioned in the deed creating said Board given by Mary Baker G. Eddy to Ira O. Knapp and others, dated September 1st, 1892, and recorded with Suffolk Deeds, Book 2081, page 257. In addition to the trusts contained in said deed of September 1, 1892, from Mary Baker G. Eddy,

this property is conveyed on the further trusts
that no new Tenet or By-Law shall be adopted,
nor any Tenet or By-Law amended or annulled
by the grantees unless the written consent of said
Mary Baker G. Eddy, the author of the textbook
" SCIENCE AND HEALTH WITH KEY TO THE SCRIP-
TURES," be given therefor, or unless at the written request of Mrs. Eddy the Executive Members
of The First Church of Christ, Scientist, (formerly called the " First Members,") by a two-
thirds vote of all their number, decide so to do.
And that the same inscription which is on the
outside of the present church edifice shall be
placed on any new church erected on said lot.
And in consideration of one dollar to me paid
by said Ira O. Knapp, William B. Johnson,
Joseph Armstrong and Stephen A. Chase, the
receipt whereof is hereby acknowledged, I do
hereby confirm the deed as above mentioned, and
do grant and release unto them, their heirs, successors and assigns in trust as aforesaid, the
premises therein described.

In Witness Whereof I have hereunto set my
hand and seal this nineteenth day of March, A. D.
nineteen hundred and three.

ALBERT METCALF. [Seal]

COMMONWEALTH OF MASSACHUSETTS
SUFFOLK } *ss.* MARCH 20th, 1903.

Then said Albert Metcalf acknowledged the foregoing instrument to be his free act and deed.

Before me

MALCOLM McLOUD.
Justice of the Peace.

MARCH 20, 1903, at twelve o'clock and sixteen minutes P. M. Received, Entered and Examined.

Attest: THOS. F. TEMPLE, *Reg.*

A true copy from the RECORDS OF DEEDS for the COUNTY OF SUFFOLK, Lib. 2886, Fol. 521.

Attest: CHAS. W. KIMBALL, *Asst. Reg.*

Topical Index

Topical Index

A

Adoption 46

Adulteration of Christian Science 43

Advising against Class Instruction 87

Announcing Author's Name 58

Annual Election (Vice-President Board of
 Education) 88

Annual Meetings 56

Applications, Approving 38

Applications for Membership 35

Applications Signed by Three Members 36

Associations 84

Associations without Teachers 86

Audit — Semi-annual 76

Authorized to Teach 86

Autopsy 50

B

Board of Directors 56, 57, 65, 67, 75, 76, 77

Board of Education 88, 89

Board of Lectureship 41, 93, 95

Books of Our Leader 27

Branch Churches, Discipline in 55

Buildings 27
Building, The Mother Church 103
Burial 50
Business Committee 79
Business of The Mother Church 27

C

Calls to Our Leader's Home 68
Cards Removed 82
Certificates 85, 90, 91
Charitable to All 48
Children 35, 46
Christ Jesus 41
Christian Fellowship 51
Church Building 102
Church Connections 34
Church Edifices 48
Church Organization 73
Circuit Lecturer 94
Circulating Literature 98
Class Teaching 87
Clerk 25
Committee on Publication 97
Communications from Our Leader 65
Communion 61
Conducting Associations 86
Confer with Teacher 88
Conferences of Churches 70
Confidences of Patients 46
Consulting M. D. 47
Controlling Students 87

Copyright 81
Corner Stone 60
Countersigning 37

D

Daily Defense 42
Daily Prayer 41
Debating 50
Degree C. S. D. 89
Democratic Government 74
Diagnoses 47
Directors 29, 30, 36, 44, 50, 51, 54, 55, 56
Directors may call for Lecture 95
Discipline 28, 33, 51, 52
Discipline by Readers 33
Discipline of Branches 55
Discussions 26
Disobedience to Church Laws 28
Disobedience to Our Leader's Orders 65
Disrespect to Our Leader 53
Donations by The Mother Church 78
Duplicate Meetings 61

E

Easter 60
Education of Readers 32
Electing Members 38
Election, Annual 88
Employees Acceptable 81
Endorsing Applications 37
English Scholars 30, 90

F

Fee, Tuition 91
Fellowship 74
Field of Labor 84
Finance Committee 76
Finance Committee, Discipline Board of
    Directors 77
Financial Situation 75
First Reader, Duties of 31
Formulas Forbidden 43
Free Instruction 91
Funds, Surplus 91

G

Gifts 67

H

Healing and Teaching 92
Hold-overs 26
Husband and Wife 92
Hypnotism Forbidden 53

I

Incorrect Literature 43
Ineligibles 39
Initials C. S. 46

L

Leader, But One 65
Lectures 95
Legal Action 67

Legal Titles 45
Lesson-Sermon 58
Librarians 63
Literature 64
Literature, Incorrect 43
Living in Harmony 51
Local Affairs 94
Local Government 70

M

Malpractice Prohibited 42
Manual 104
Manual, re Branches 72
Marriage Ceremony 49
Matthew 18:15–17 51
Meetings, Board of Directors 57
Meetings, No Duplicates 61
Member must Believe 34
Membership essential 92
Members' Meeting called by Clerk 57
Men, generally 99
Misrepresenting Our Leader 54
Monopoly of Field 49
Mother Church Lectures 95
Mother, Title of, Changed 64
Music 61

N

Name, Announcing Author's 59
Name, " Without the Life " 50
Naming Author 32

Net Profits 80
No Malpractice 42
No Monopoly 49
No New Laws 105
No one Teacher 73
No Remarks 32
No Revision of Manual 105
Normal Students 37
Notices 32
Numbering the People 48
Number of Pupils 84
Nurses 49

O

Objectionable Pictures 81
Obnoxious Books 44
Obstetrics Not Taught 88
Officers 25
Offices in Reading Room 74
Officious Members 45
One Christ 42
Organization 44
Organizing Churches 72
Other Organizations 45
Other Vocations 82
Our Leader to be Consulted 70

P

Paper on Practice and Malpractice 90
Pastor Emeritus 26, 29, 30
Pastor, Our 58

Per Capita Tax 44
Periodicals 44
Petty Cash, Treasurer 78
Practising Wrongly 55
Practitioners and Patients 46
Prayer in Church 42
President 25
Prices Reduced 46
Primary Class 90
Probationary 38
Public Topics 93
Publication Committee 27, 29, 78, 82
Publishing Society Trustees 79
Publishing without Consent 82
Pupils of Strayed Teachers 85

R

Readers 26, 29
Readers, Removing 30
Readers, Residence 30
Reading Rooms 63
Rejection of Members 37
Removal by Board of Directors 100
Restoring Members 39
Rule for Motives and Acts 40

S

Salary 29
Services 60
Seventy-third Edition 104
Societies, Other 45

Soliciting Pupils 87
Sue, Patients 46
Suitable Employees 81
Sunday-School Teaching 62
Surplus Funds 91
Syndicates 27

T

Teacher, Not to Control 83
Teacher, On Probation 55
Teachers, Disloyal, etc. 36
Teach from Recapitulation 86
Teaching, Motive for 83
Teaching Roman Catholics 87
Teaching Wrongly 55
Tenets Copyrighted 71
Term of Office 80
Testimonials 47
Three Years with Our Leader 91
Title " The " 70
Titles to be Dropped 45
Treasurer 25
Trustees, Publishing Society 79
Tuition Fee 84

U

Unique, The Mother Church 71
Universities and Colleges 73
Unjust Articles 53
Unspotted from World 31

V

Vacancies 80, 89
Violation of By-Laws 50
Visitors in Sunday School 62
Visitors Welcomed, The Mother Church 59

W

Wednesday Evening Meetings 31
Welcoming Visitors 59
Wide Channels 45
Wisdom, Economy, and Brotherly Love 77
Withdrawals 38
Women, Publication Committee 100
Working against Cause 52
Wrong Practice 55
Wrong Teaching 55

THE PLIMPTON PRESS, NORWOOD, MASS., U.S.A.